FLIPPING THE SWITCH

FLIPPING

— THE —

SWITCH

HOW WE STARTED AND SCALED

A GLOBAL LIGHTING BRAND

COLE ZUCKER | GUILLAUME VIDAL

LIONCREST
PUBLISHING

FLIPPING THE SWITCH
How We Started and Scaled a Global Lighting Brand
First Edition

ISBN   978-1-5445-4404-5   *Hardcover*
       978-1-5445-4403-8   *Paperback*
       978-1-5445-4402-1   *Ebook*
       978-1-5445-4405-2   *Audiobook*

CONTENTS

Preface   **xi**

A Chance Meeting   **1**

Tracking Opportunity   **9**

Seeing the Market Firsthand   **19**

Quitting   **23**

Confirming Our Suspicions   **27**

Developing My Competitive Advantage   **33**

My Time of Discovery   **41**

Subcontracting and Setting Up Shop   **49**

In San Francisco It Was Hustle or Die   **61**

All the Little Details   **65**

All the Noes Before a Yes   **73**

Always in Lean Mode   **89**

Getting to the End User and Our First Big Sale   **95**

Learning the Market on the Move   **103**

Our First Distributor   **115**

Meeting the Market   **119**

Building a Sales Team   **125**

Managing on the China Side   **139**

The First Big Sale and the Momentum That Followed   **153**

New Products   **161**

Lessons in Hiring   **165**

Logistics for an International Company   **169**

Validation from the Outside   **175**

Our First Major Supply Chain Issue   **183**

New Distributors, New Customers, and a New Direction   **189**

Going Premium   **201**

Sticking to the Vision and Doubling the Team   **213**

A New Office and Finding Our Categories   **223**

Finding the Right Partners and People   **233**

What Comes with Growth   **249**

It Was Time to Sell   **261**

An End and a Beginning   **269**

What You Can't Prepare For   **273**

Final Note to the Reader   **277**

PREFACE

Entrepreneurship is one heck of a ride. Just thinking about walking away from a steady salary to explore the great unknown can make your hands feel sweaty. And the first few years can be especially tough as you are met with waves of rejection and struggle to find product/market fit.

And for those, like us, who were bootstrapped, watching your personal bank account decline month after month is a gut-wrenching experience. It's hard to not look at yourself in the mirror each morning and question your decision.

But then there's the other side—after you've recognized the market opportunity, after you've put in countless hours for no pay, and after you've finally capitalized on what began as a seed of an idea. The payoff can be truly life-altering.

In talking with many entrepreneurs, we've found that our journeys are strikingly similar. One consistent theme that many entrepreneurs experience is learning through failure. Whether it's making the wrong strategic decision or a bad hire, or mismanaging your cash flow, there are countless lessons to learn.

We've made more mistakes than we care to admit, but it's how we bounced back and avoided repeating those mistakes that made us successful.

In sharing our story, we hope not only to inspire but to help other entrepreneurs navigate the complex and challenging world of starting and scaling a business.

We started our company with limited capital, knowledge, and experience. But we committed ourselves to giving everything we could to it. And now we can proudly say that we founded and scaled a global LED (light emitting diode) lighting brand in GREEN CREATIVE.

So buckle up, grab a cup of coffee (or a stiff drink), and get ready to learn from our mistakes, our successes, and everything in between. Because if we can do it, so can you!

A CHANCE MEETING

COLE

We met at a Mexican restaurant in China.

When I first saw Guillaume, all I could focus on was the goofy sweater this French guy wore. It was this Steve Jobs–esque black turtleneck. The neckline almost hit his chin.

Must be a French thing, I thought.

When the group wrapped up dinner, the night was still young, and we all headed to a club. I settled onto a bar stool. I ordered and was waiting on my drink when someone came up and pushed me from behind. Without hesitation, Guillaume jumped off his stool, grabbed the guy, and pushed him back.

I like this guy, I remember thinking. He barely knew me, but he literally had my back.

We spoke for the remainder of the night, and, as we chatted, we realized we had quite a bit in common. We were both peripherally involved in the lighting industry, and we both had cars, which was rare among foreigners in Shanghai.

Unfortunately, this commonality wasn't notable enough for us to stay in touch. While we exchanged numbers, we quickly moved on, caught up in the momentum of life—girlfriends, work, and the day-to-day. Our initial spark faded into a fond memory. I assumed Guillaume had left China. Shanghai was transient by nature. Our mutual friend who'd connected us had left six months previously, so it would've been no surprise if Guillaume had followed suit.

———

I'd come to China to start a business that I could bring home to the US. The seeds of this idea were planted at a young age. When I was growing up, my grandfather frequently reminded me of China's coming importance on the global scale, citing how it had recently joined the

World Trade Organization. "The 2000s will be considered the Chinese Century," he'd say. "It will be defined by China's modernization and domination of the planet."

His advice: learn Mandarin and get to China.

But China was far from the suburbs of New Jersey, and I was in no hurry to leave the comforts of home. Even when it was time to go to college, I chose a school just an hour away so I could still visit family.

But even with this proximity to home, college opened my eyes and ignited a desire to travel, explore, and see what the world had to offer. My first opportunity to travel was in my junior year. As a business major, I was encouraged to study for a semester abroad. While the rest of my classmates debated the options, I knew where I'd go.

———

It was 2003 when I landed in Beijing for the first time. The city was getting prepared for the 2008 Summer Olympics. Construction was everywhere. For three months, I interned at a local real estate developer and interacted as much as possible with the locals. By the time I returned to the US, I'd learned enough Mandarin to greet someone and ask them where I could find the nearest bathroom.

While it wasn't quite enough to start a multilingual international company, more important than greetings and toilet-based queries was the commitment I made to return. My grandfather was right. China was the land of opportunity, and I could feel it.

———

In 2006, a year after graduating college, I landed a job on Wall Street at a large financial services corporation. There were no ties to China, but the salary was terrific, and I could see myself moving up the management track. It was the beginning of a safe, secure, lucrative future. It was every college graduate's dream. But it wasn't mine.

Days spent entering data into Excel models and validating numbers didn't do much for me. There was no adventure, no ownership in the work, and no joy. I hated the job, and it hated me back. Soon enough, I got the boot.

Reluctantly, I began, once again, the interview process, but nothing spoke to me. All the jobs looked the same— row after row of cubicles and desks and monitors and people who seemed bored out of their skulls. It wasn't the life I wanted. I began to realize that, up until that point, I'd let fear dictate my path. I was dissatisfied, and it was time to listen to a different voice. I could hear one. I had no idea if it was one of insanity or bravery or heart, but I knew I had to at least give my dream a shot.

So I bought a one-way ticket, sold almost everything I owned, stuffed the rest into a couple of duffle bags, and headed to Shanghai. I had no job lined up and little savings. All I had was a belief in myself that I could make something work.

———

I found a job as a sales agent, working for a building materials manufacturer in Shanghai. I spent my days traveling to large construction projects across China, calling on contractors and end users to get them to purchase our products. However, my real purpose for moving to China was to do something entrepreneurial. I began to develop some ideas on the side.

I tried to create advertising magazines, which were essentially coupon books, but that didn't work out. I tried to make eye drops that cooled one's eyes, but when I finally found a manufacturer, they informed me it was already in every Rite Aid around the US, manufactured through a global Japanese brand. Next, I turned my focus to alternative construction materials. The plan was to sell magnesium panels to builders. A friend with a pillow business had attended a conference and returned with $2 million in orders. Inspired by his success and an "I can do it too" attitude, I flew to Frankfurt, Germany, for a construction conference. I hit the showroom floor with the confidence that my future was in that room. Unfortunately, my high hopes were soon dashed. I wandered the convention floor, handing out product flyers to people who spoke no English and, if they had, likely wouldn't have wanted to speak with me.

The failed attempts hit hard. My boss had the money and nice cars I lacked. I felt like beyond the material aspects, there was little that separated us. I had the appetite for risk, the determination, and the work ethic, but a piece was still missing. Then, one day, I found it.

———

It was a particularly bad Wednesday. From six in the morning on, I struggled to keep up. By five o'clock, I'd made seven sales calls and had many more to do by the end of the week.

The drive home wasn't any better. It was a stop-and-go crawl. Rush hour in 2010 Shanghai was no joke. To my misfortune, I'd had no choice but to grow accustomed to it in the three years since I'd arrived. It was a problem that had no immediate solution. City planners had underestimated the number of people who'd have cars. Parking was even more of a nightmare. I arrived home and circled the block around my apartment building for what felt like an eternity.

Finally, I found a spot and trudged to my building, through the lobby, and into the elevator. With a slight lurch, it began its long journey to the 23rd floor.

The doors slid open. Rest was within reach. I'd survived another day, and as I opened the door to my 800-square-foot apartment and flopped down on the couch, the TV flashed to life and there was Guillaume eating a waffle. It was the French guy with the goofy sweater.

I hadn't seen him in months, but there he was on my TV, in an interview with a local news station.

Had my exhaustion finally caught up to me?

Was it really him?

Why was he eating a waffle?

Had fate finally intervened?

While fate hadn't intervened for the waffle shop (it was a PR stunt, and Guillaume's friend owned the franchise), it might have intervened for me.

I'd never watched the local news, and I'd set the TV to the Philippines cable network—the nearest English-speaking programming. My butt had done the work of turning on the TV for me. Maybe this would be a good day after all.

I sprang off the sofa, grabbed my phone, and sent him a text that would change the course of our lives.

TRACKING
OPPORTUNITY

GUILLAUME

Hey, Guillaume! I just saw you on TV. Crazy. What are you up to these days?

I responded almost immediately. The timing was perfect. Come 2010, I was two years into working as a product manager at a factory that manufactured lighting. My boss was incredible and so were my colleagues. The only problem was that I'd reached the limit of my growth. Customers and friends kept telling me I should start my own business. It was time to search for a new way forward. The signs were there, and my entrepreneurial spirit was at an all-time high. So when Cole reached out, I won-dered if the universe had finally found a way to reach me.

We quickly set a meeting, and in a matter of days, we were swapping stories over whiskey and green tea at the neon-lit and heavily chandeliered 88 Club in Shanghai. It didn't take long before I realized that there was a mutual opportunity between us. The meeting seemed to hold weight. I could almost feel it; my life was about to change in a big way. We simply clicked. We were both tired of working for others and were ready to set out on our own. The only caveat was that Cole wanted to move back to the US and I wanted to stay in China. But a solution immedi-ately presented itself. We wondered if this, too, could play to our advantage. If Cole could be successful in sales in China, I had no doubt he could be even more successful in his home country. Perhaps we had a winning partner-ship on our hands. We had, quite literally, arrived from opposite sides of the world, but our visions seemed per-fectly aligned.

———

Becoming business partners wasn't something we decided to do over a single drink. There wasn't one moment where we said, "Yes, let's start a business together." It was more of a natural progression.

We shared similar perspectives on life. We both saw China as a country of entrepreneurs. It was a culture that resonated with us. We understood the importance of taking risks and were willing to mess up and try again. This made us different from most people. We could've stayed comfortable—in the New York finance world or the French countryside—but instead we seized the opportunity to travel, pursue new ideas, and learn a new language. That willingness to take risks, to step outside our comfort zones, was what created the circumstances for us to even meet in the first place.

We explored the ways we might work together, and as we did, our complementary skills continued to become more apparent. But our compatibility went beyond our skillsets. We lived similar lifestyles. Neither of us had kids or a family, so we weren't goaded by the need for a serious salary, nor were we distracted by volatile relationships or personal issues. We could prioritize a new business and commit ourselves 100 percent.

As we moved forward in our conversations, we felt like we were moving further from the edge into deeper waters.

We still had our full-time jobs, but a path to becoming full-time entrepreneurs was on the horizon. To build anything, you need a foundation and clarity, and the more we discussed, the closer we got to figuring out what our business was going to be. We knew it'd be lighting related, but we didn't know what the model would look like. We had to discover what would be beyond the horizon.

———

Thankfully, we had a head start when it came to identifying our business model. In our current jobs, we were both able to see how the lighting industry was changing. LED lights were going to become the dominant technology, disrupting the existing technologies on the market. We wanted to be a part of LED's disruptive force. The question was, what would be the best way to enter the market?

Our first idea was to lease LED lights to companies. Under this model, we'd give the lights away for free and charge a percentage of the savings they made from switching to LED.

It didn't take us long to realize that this was a messy business model. It was easy to imagine the phone ringing off the hook with complaints about broken lights or requests for bill adjustments. And if that wasn't enough, to get paid correctly, we'd have to trace every light we leased. It all felt like a headache to manage and sustain, and we hadn't even started.

We turned our attention to the retail market. A product in Home Depot or Walmart seemed like the best possible option, and it didn't take a genius to recognize that the volume could be huge with this model. On the flip side, the risk was high. Going retail meant we'd be competing with large established brands. Not to mention, it would be challenging to land a place on the shelf, and all the work might be worth nothing if they got rid of them a year later. One wave of returns could kill the business. All around, it was a business model filled with liabilities. We decided to let the big manufacturers do their deals with retailers. We didn't want to fight an uphill battle from day one.

We then considered trading and selling to importers. The idea was to be the middleman, selling directly to local markets on behalf of manufacturers for a percentage of each purchase as a service fee. But, once again, the model didn't make much sense from a long-term perspective. We wanted to grow, and the potential here felt capped.

One key insight we had was that LED was going to be a race to the sockets. LED lifetimes were so long that once they were in a socket, you wouldn't sell a replacement for at least five years.

We realized that our best chance at success was to start a brand that built and sold LED lights. We'd be in the commercial market. No retail. No leasing. With this model, we'd need to partner with suppliers who had factories and tools to build the products, but at the end of the day, we'd be considered the manufacturer, and we'd be able to compete against the big brands like Philips. Because we were a new brand, we'd have to price our products well below the major players to gain market traction, but we knew that over time we could establish ourselves as a player and grow.

We had our business model in hand, and it was time to make this dream a reality.

The following months were filled with dreams and ambitions about how we'd take the lighting market by storm. Our energy was frenetic. The business consumed us. Each second counted. Every weekend morning, I'd order McDonald's Egg McMuffins for delivery, timed so breakfast would arrive around the same time as Cole.

TO BE AN ENTREPRENEUR, YOU MUST ALWAYS LOOK AHEAD

So much of our process, even from the start, was about spotting the opportunity and taking it. When it came to an initial idea, the key thing to consider was the potential. In the startup world, this is called TAM (total addressable market). When getting started, we had to ask ourselves if our business idea was attacking a market big enough for us to get a sizable piece. If we'd pursued a market that was relatively small, it would have been much more challenging to scale the business.

When we first began discussing our strategy, the LED lighting industry was on the cusp of exploding into a huge market—prices were still too high, technology was nascent, and there hadn't yet been an S-curve adoption. Back then, we knew what was coming, though, and we knew that it would be the best time to establish a brand. LED lighting at the time was growing at 15 percent per year, and it would become a $20 billion market in the US. We wanted to be part of its growth.

Our experience shows that you can be a new entrant in a fast-growing industry, especially if you can anticipate the future and adapt your products better than the established players.

We'd immediately get to work, pausing only to get an unbeatable pesto penne for lunch across the street at Wagas (a midpriced restaurant chain that served some delicious foreign food). We finished these days exhausted with the excitement of knowing that we were on the precipice of a new chapter in our personal and professional lives. It was more than a dream. We had critical pieces of our foundation in place, but one piece we didn't have was a name. We struggled to find something that clicked.

We decided to try to make a few small decisions, which would hopefully lead us to a bigger one. We thought the name should include both a G and a C, for Guillaume and Cole, and we wanted to come across as a tech company that manufactured LED lights, not a lighting company dipping its toe into the LED business. Ideally, the name would evoke a green element. In 2010, most people weren't aware that LED lighting was, in fact, a green product. The idea was that if we referenced it in our name, it would help key people into that fact.

One day, we were sitting on my apartment balcony, brainstorming our name for what felt like the hundredth time, when, finally, two words came to mind.

"GREEN CREATIVE," I said.

Cole looked over at me, a smile on his face. "Wow," he said. "That's perfect."

———

The next step was to make a logo. There were a lot of lighting companies that had green in their name and logo colors, which made them look less like tech companies (or even lighting companies, for that matter) and more like conservancy groups. We wanted to appear as a forward-facing tech company, so we settled on dark gray and blue, with our initials interlocking to look like a power button.

The logo ended up giving us an unexpected perk, especially early on. When someone saw it, they'd inevitably ask, "Why is your logo blue and white, but your name uses 'green'?" It gave us a chance to explain our reasoning, which would help connect the ideas with the image.

GREEN CREATIVE was coming to life.

SEEING THE MARKET FIRSTHAND

COLE

You've got to come down here. This is crazy.

It was a text from Guillaume.

At the start of the week, he'd flown to southern China to attend the Guangzhou International Lighting Exhibition, one of the biggest lighting exhibitions on the planet.

Until this point, neither of us had compromised our day jobs to work on the business. We were still in ideation mode, meeting at night and on weekends. But this was a moment of truth. I was at work, and Guillaume was asking me to get on a plane on a Wednesday. If I went, I'd miss the next two days of work without notice.

I looked up from my desk. My coworkers buzzed around the office. I saw where I was and where I wanted to be. I looked back at the phone. Was I about to take the leap?

Just booked my flight, I typed out.

I pressed send and booked my ticket.

On the drive to the airport that night, I could feel something new happening. We were moving past ideas and into action. If Guillaume was asking me to take this two-and-a-half-hour trip, he felt it was important. And it was.

Talking about the market and seeing it firsthand are two very different things. The exhibition opened our eyes to the breadth of the lighting industry and served as the perfect means of aligning our understanding and vision. We saw all the opportunities for subcontracting. Businesses and vendors brought not only their current product lines but also upcoming products that their R&D (research and development) departments were developing. Understanding the technologies provided us with a significant advantage as we moved toward building our products, and this was the place to learn. There were walls of product in every booth as far as the eye could see. We were surrounded by burgeoning technology and leaders in the space and were able to discuss and truly entertain our business. Guillaume's knowledge shined through, and we spoke to many of his valuable contacts. Only now, we spoke to them as if we were also players in the industry because we were. And we'd seen our opening.

Among the hundreds of manufacturers in attendance, maybe 20 percent of the products on display were LEDs. These weren't even full lines. They were more or less prototypes. Nothing was ready for mass production. These were the early days, most companies lacked the capacity, ability, and understanding of where the market was going, and a majority of the LEDs on display didn't look particularly great. They had a space-age vibe that brought with it the subtle promise of the future combined with the general consensus that they still weren't at a place to replace existing lighting technology, at least not yet. Halogen, incandescent, and CFL still ruled the market, and the output of LEDs only enticed early adopters who were curious about the technology. Still, we felt one thing was clear: LED would become a viable product. It was just a matter of time. And those who were willing to step into those unknown waters would likely benefit most.

For the first time, it was more than just a concept. We were face-to-face with the future and ready to make it our own.

QUITTING

GUILLAUME

By June 2010, we'd been working on our ideas and new business for months. We'd assembled a pitch deck, created a simple operating agreement, and even gone to Hong Kong to open a bank account. Google became our third business partner as we relied heavily on search to help us figure out how to start a business.

At that point, we had as clear a vision as we could, and it seemed like there was only one more thing to do: quit.

We both still had our day jobs, with deadlines we needed to meet on a regular basis. We began to feel the squeeze and knew we couldn't keep up the pace for much longer. We both committed to quitting by December 31.

This was a major step that required an enormous level of trust. After all, we didn't actually have a company yet. We didn't have even one cent in the bank from the business. Still, we knew this was our only choice. We had to go all in and take the leap.

In my job, I oversaw about 75 percent of the products in the factory. I was involved in R&D and sourcing, and I managed a lot of people. Because of my position, and because I didn't want to burn any bridges, I knew I couldn't give a simple two weeks' notice. So I gave six months' notice instead, letting my boss know I'd leave by the end of the year.

As soon as I told him, he said, "We're not surprised. We knew you'd start your own company at some point. Just promise me we can partner with you down the road."

His words gave me a boost of confidence, and I was happy to promise a continued relationship. I knew we'd need equipment for testing new products, and now I knew just where to turn.

———

Without our day jobs, we'd have more time to build the business together, but we'd lose out on income. It was simultaneously thrilling and terrifying. It was a dive into the deep waters with the shallows barely in sight.

After calculating our combined money, we realized we needed to downsize, and ASAP.

At the time, I lived in a fancy 1,000-square-foot apartment in Shanghai with a balcony that overlooked the city. My new apartment was three times smaller and, later that year, I realized I couldn't afford any apartment in Shanghai. I needed to move outside the city center. The residential complex I ultimately ended up at was so big—accommodating almost 10,000 people—that I couldn't even find my apartment when I first moved, and when I sheepishly asked the security guard for help, he simply smiled. For him, this was nothing new.

We also downsized our everyday spending. During our early meetings, we'd eat out regularly. We'd go to fancy restaurants. I'd order delivery almost daily. But there could be no more of that. I brought my budget down by 75 percent. At first, we tried to still eat something a bit more upscale on occasion, but eventually, we simply didn't have the money. The local rice and noodle shops would have to do.

For me, the biggest change was connected to partying. When Cole and I first met, I went out several times a week and spent an embarrassing amount each night. Once we started the business, I knew I couldn't keep it up. At first, my friends insisted, "Don't worry. We'll cover you." But after four or five times of hitting the town without money, it was time for these nights to come to an end. These evenings were already spent worrying about their cost despite my friends' insistence it was no issue, so it wasn't a huge change.

No longer going out, if I wanted to drink, I opted for supermarket beer, but more often than not, I settled for nothing at all. And there were benefits to this. I no longer had to reserve the weekends for recovery, and cutting out alcohol allowed for more efficient time management on the weekend. However, I'd be lying if I didn't acknowledge that it did impact some friendships. When you cut out drinking, you unfortunately realize that a lot of friendships and relationships revolve around places to eat and drink. That part was hard. After all, Shanghai is an amazing place, particularly for young single men.

These shifts in lifestyle set me up for the next stage in building the business. Soon there'd be no room for partying. We'd need all hands on deck all the time.

CONFIRMING OUR SUSPICIONS

COLE

Four months after the exhibition, I'd quit my job and was planning a trip back to the US for Thanksgiving and my best friend's bachelor party. I looked forward to the wedding, but I was primarily thrilled by the opportunity to investigate the potential for the LED market in the US. Our connections were in China and Europe, and the US felt like a blind spot, which was a problem since I hoped to bring the business back to the States and make it our primary market for sales.

Before I left, Guillaume shared an article with me that stated that Japan's LED bulbs had recently surpassed its CFL bulbs (the curly-Q fluorescent bulbs that nobody likes). It predicted that the inflection point for switching to LED in the US would come in two years and that currently there were eight billion light sockets in the US ready to be converted.

I was pumped and ready to investigate. America awaited.

———

I made the most of my trip to the United States. While we hopped from Philadelphia bar to strip club to bar for my friend's bachelor party, I spent most of the evening focusing on the lights—every outlet, every sconce, every streetlight. Unsurprisingly, they were everywhere. It's hard to see without them.

At each turn, there was another light ripe for conversion. I felt like Sherlock Holmes, committed to the case of the missing LEDs, but there were none to be found. A market was there. Now, this certainly wasn't scientific market research, but it did plenty to convince me that our instincts were correct.

———

Before I returned to China, I took the time to chat with a few connections in the lighting industry. At this point, we'd put together a fundraising deck, and I hoped I might find some investors while I was there. We called anyone in our network who could write a check, no matter how small.

Everyone said no. They couldn't understand why we'd try to compete with GE or Philips.

Even if we had raised some money at this point, we knew it wouldn't be enough. We'd still be forced to do everything necessary to maximize our runway. But now, with zero money raised, there was only one choice before us: we had to believe in ourselves. So we took our life savings, opened a bank account in Hong Kong, and wired all our money into the joint account.

———

On the flight back to China, I was excited to tell Guillaume what I'd found. Not only was our idea viable, but also our brand would be on the cutting edge before the LED wave hit.

I thought of the stories Guillaume had told me about large lighting companies—the layers they had to go through to get a new product developed. If we could approach the market like a technology company, we'd be way ahead of the game. Philips, GE, and other legacy players would likely act like Ford and GM did when electric cars came on the scene; they'd transition slowly, and by the time they launched, we could be on to our second and third generations.

There was an opening, and our future looked bright.

The final piece of our foundation that we needed was the company structure. We already had a sense of it, but we wrote it down to make things official.

We divided roles by skillset. China would be our hub for manufacturing, where Guillaume would oversee the R&D, subcontracting, quality, testing, certification, merchandising, and marketing. The US would be our market, where I'd set up sales, customer support, warehousing, and finance.

Many international companies operate with their corporate office in one location and satellite offices in others. With this model, you have a CEO or a central figure who manages the entire team, no matter their location. We didn't see a need to centralize like this, especially when we wanted to build a multicontinental business. To us, the China side and the US side had two distinct functions.

SOMETIMES TO LEARN TO SWIM, YOU SIMPLY NEED TO JUMP INTO THE WATER

There was nothing sophisticated about our approach. A lot of people talk about wanting to be an entrepreneur, but they aren't willing to take the plunge. This doesn't mean you don't start slow at the shallow end. After all, a drowning man doesn't ever have much of a chance. But the point is this: more action and less thinking keeps you moving one way or another. And the truth is that you'll inevitably have to learn as you go anyway, so why fight it?

Sure, we got turned down by a lot of people initially, but some of those same people would later reach out to us and tell us they made a big mistake. It wasn't that they were wrong, of course. We didn't have the money or resources we needed. But what they couldn't see was our belief in learning and finding a way to stay afloat.

From a leadership perspective, we'd be co-CEOs with highly defined roles and responsibilities in two separate locations. The benefit of this model was that we could scale the company with two key leaders instead of one, and we could think and move together each step of the way.

This strategic positioning from a global perspective would be the first of our unfair advantages. The second was our existing knowledge of the lighting industry and our combined understanding of manufacturing, R&D, marketing, and sales.

DEVELOPING MY COMPETITIVE ADVANTAGE

GUILLAUME

When I first met Cole, I was working at a factory in Shanghai. The knowledge and skills I gained there had a huge impact on our success. My work there taught me a new perspective on the business, not only on the manufacturing but also on the higher-value parts that came into play further down the line. My road to Shanghai, however, was less direct than this transfer of skills.

I grew up in Mende, a city in the Lozère department, in what's known as the French Desert. However, in reality, it's less of a desert and more of a green-filled space high in the mountains, roughly 3,000 feet above sea level. The name comes from its small population, and while most people who grow up there never leave, I was one of the lucky few who escaped to take on the world.

As a boy, I was mesmerized by my dad's business. I wanted to try entrepreneurship for myself. At ten, I went house to house with dried lavender bags and left with cash in hand. At 16, I ran a small DJ business, doing music for weddings and other events. Throughout all of this, somehow I found time to work for my dad's business—making copies, delivering office furniture, and learning some of the ins and outs of entrepreneurship along the way. My favorite part of it all was the adrenaline of making my own money and then making more.

Despite my entrepreneurial endeavors, I didn't do so well in school. I remember my mom frequently saying, "Guillaume, at least take your book bag off your scooter so I think you're studying." But we both knew there'd be no studying.

In France, students choose a course of advanced study before entering high school. I wanted to be a motorbike mechanic, so I chose engineering. After a year, I decided that I actually wanted to become a fighter jet pilot, but my math and physics scores were less than ideal. So, to get through high school, I shifted to sales. It was the perfect course of study for someone who didn't study.

After high school, I joined a two-year associate's degree program in marketing and sales. I didn't do well. I spent too much time doing everything other than studying. I wanted to quit, but my father gave me an ultimatum: I could move back home, but I'd have to work for him again and contribute to rent and food, or I could return to school.

This ultimatum lit a fire under me. I returned to school, got to work, and ended my second year as the top student in the class. After graduation, all I knew was that I wanted to experience more of the world. So I followed my girlfriend to Ireland, off to the next adventure, where I discovered the limitations of my knowledge of English.

In Ireland, I began two daily habits to strengthen my English. Every evening, I read ten pages of a book written in English. I had to look up so many words it often took me more than an hour. After this grating task, I'd watch an episode of *The Simpsons*. This was much less stressful and, honestly, the more helpful of the two. Homer and his family talked like regular people, not like a textbook. If my homework in school had been *The Simpsons*, I would've already been much further along.

Ireland was also where I discovered a way to keep traveling. Funnily enough, it was a few French exchange students who showed me the way: an advanced business degree. Thankfully, due to all the schooling I already had, I only had to pass an exam and choose a school on the French Riviera, the Silicon Valley of France, but after my second year, I again felt restless. I wasn't pushing my limits enough, and I knew it was time to get out of the country again. I came across a six-month opportunity in Hong Kong. I'd never considered Asia as an option, but when the exchange program counselor at the school showed me photographs of the campus, which sits on a hill overlooking a private beach, I was hooked. It was less of a college campus and more of a resort. *Just the right kind of school for me*, I thought.

This program felt like an initiation into business and adulthood. I was immersed in a new world. I lived in a shared bedroom on campus with another student, forced myself to speak English as often as possible, and did everything I could to avoid anyone French. I was determined to live the dream I'd seen on American TV, the real "campus life," and I did. The first time out with the other exchange students, I was punched in the face. I was alive in ways I'd never felt before.

I loved the experience so much that I argued with my school to let me make my final presentation remotely. If I flew back to France, I wouldn't be able to afford my flight back. Thankfully, I was able to stay.

By the end of this time, I had a business degree and some amazing new friends—exchange students from Canada, Mexico, and the Netherlands. As soon as we graduated, we all decided to visit Southeast Asia. In the middle of our trip, I received an email from a man in Hong Kong who wanted to interview me for a paid internship at a trading company. After a successful interview, I got my first job. I was 24 and living in Hong Kong. The feeling was exhilarating, to say the least.

The job itself was a training ground. I worked for a French trading company, helping companies who didn't have an office in Asia purchase products in China, monitor manufacturing, and inspect and ship goods. I enjoyed the work, and two and a half years in, my boss asked me if I'd like to open a new office in Shanghai.

Shanghai was a whole different world. Up until this point, I'd avoided the mainland. It was still developing, and if I took the job, I'd have to learn a new language and adapt to a new culture. I would also be making less since the cost of living was cheaper in Mainland China. This was clearly no small choice. In the end, I decided to take the opportunity. No matter what happened, I knew I'd gain something invaluable: experience. So, still broke, I made my way to Shanghai.

The move opened more opportunities to learn than I could've imagined. Within a year, I learned to hire, fire, and keep all the parts of the office running smoothly while trying to keep some sort of sanity too. Little did I know then that this was perfect practice for the actual act of starting a business. It was an entrepreneurial experience under someone else's checking account. It was an exciting time. I was working on big projects with big brands.

After about 18 months in Shanghai, I switched my focus at the trading company from buying and selling products from different vendors to actually working for one of the vendors—a fast-growing lighting factory outside of Shanghai that worked with global retailers and brands. I was in charge of product management. I worked

with R&D and engineers. I dealt with sourcing and manufacturing and visited parts vendors. This was my first
look beyond the glossy sales and presentation side of the
industry. I witnessed the complexity of the business. I
began to develop an understanding for the sourcing of
all the parts, components, and finished products; warehousing for components or finished goods; marketing,
with all the design and work for customers and company;
manufacturing with assembly; coordination of the work-
shop; R&D; and quality control.

These experiences set us up for success. But, through
all this, perhaps the most important lesson I learned was
not to spend time on things other people could do better
than me.

MY TIME OF DISCOVERY

COLE

Like Guillaume, I learned a great deal by simply taking the next step in life and seeing what I found. I didn't know it then, but all the accumulated knowledge would eventually play a pivotal role in our business together.

I first landed in Shanghai in June of 2007, three years before we started GREEN CREATIVE. I got off the plane, booked myself a bed in a hostel, and started to hustle.

It felt like I was in San Francisco during the 19th-century gold rush. There were no frills, and I loved every minute of it.

China had opened to foreign business and investment in 1978 and was growing into a manufacturing hub. By this point, the country had been developing for about 25 years, and it was becoming recognized around the globe as more than just a factory floor for the planet. The agrarian society was rapidly changing, and cities were developing fast. It was an ideal place to build and develop products.

Fifty years prior to my arrival, Mao had set the country on fire. He stamped out the proletariat class, as well as the wealthy and educated, in order to allow the migrant farmworkers to come up and equalize society. This fueled China's communism, but it also destroyed countless artifacts and relics of the past.

I remember visiting the Ming tombs in Beijing, where the royalty of the Ming dynasty was buried. The grounds were gorgeous and well maintained. When you entered the tombs, you felt like you were navigating a maze. You wound your way down, and once you arrived, there was nothing but tape on the ground where the tombs used to be. It was nothing more than an empty room. When prompted, tour guides explained that teenagers burned everything down in the 1950s as part of the cleansing of the past.

This new revolution of the 2000s looked different from the work of Mao, but the government still pushed for progress at a relentless rate. Historical neighborhoods were torn down as skyscrapers shot up. Millions of people were moving to Shanghai. Many undocumented workers traveled to the city from all across the country. It was no wonder that driving and even walking were games played at your own risk. If you simply crossed the road when the light was green, you'd promptly get knocked over. You had to know exactly when to brave the crossing and then be quick about it.

The government worked diligently to keep things together as it built and internationalized the country's presence. But when I arrived in Shanghai, there was still a roughness around its edges, and the city burst with potential. Fake goods saturated the streets. At every corner, someone waited to pawn off replica watches and pirated DVDs. Brothels masqueraded as hair salons. A market the size of a football stadium housed stalls that sold fake goods seven days a week. Ten years later, that same area would turn into an extremely expensive shopping mall.

I explored this new normal for the first three months, living out of duffle bags and networking my face off. I had to get in front of as many people as possible, hopefully people willing to hire me and launch my career. One of the people I met didn't give me a job, but he did give me an idea. "Why don't you print out your résumé and go to the financial district during lunchtime," he suggested. "Hand it out and say that you're available to work. A lot of foreigners work there already, so you won't stick out like a sore thumb."

I took his advice and headed to Xintiandi and to Pudong, two areas of the city where many financial firms had their offices. I looked for foreigners and tried to get them to take my résumé. If I even managed to catch someone's attention, I was met as though I was a crazy person accosting them on the street. But I kept at it. Getting hired would take moxie. I had to put myself out there and be willing to be rejected. It was the only way to differentiate myself from the countless candidates looking to work in the same field.

After a few months, however, the networking paid off. I met a Chinese factory owner who invited me to join his growing company. Up to that point, he'd employed only local Chinese people, but he thought that I might be an asset to the team.

His company made building materials, and I felt like this was a good time to be in that business. The country had just passed a rule that allowed foreign companies who built R&D facilities in their Chinese factories to avoid paying taxes for several years. This was a sweetheart deal for American businesses that had been manufacturing products in China but retained R&D in their own countries, especially since the US was also in the middle of a financial crisis. The tax incentive spurred companies like Microsoft and Coca-Cola to hire local contractors and engineers at new facilities in China for less than what they'd pay workers in the United States. Soon construction and hiring were booming.

I joined the company as a salesperson and stayed for three and a half years. The owner and I weren't sure, initially, how the arrangement would work out since I was an American and all his clients were Chinese. But my ability to get in front of the right people and sell turned out to be a huge asset.

Being a foreigner also paid off. I would cold-call a client and give them my pitch in Mandarin. They'd inevitably ask, "Are you a foreigner?" When I told them I was from New Jersey, they'd want to meet in person. Sometimes

I'd show up and the client would have their spouse with them just to meet the foreign salesman.

Over time, I became a novelty of sorts to attract customers, and before long, I ran the entire sales team.

At the time, Chinese companies didn't have a lot of layers. Flatter organizations, devoid of the typical business structure with its many midlevel managers, allowed an ambitious employee like me to move up quickly. So, here I was in my midtwenties, managing people and getting experience that likely wouldn't have been accessible in the US.

WHEN YOU PUSH YOURSELF OUTSIDE YOUR COMFORT ZONE, YOU FIND TREASURE

Perhaps this lesson is a prompt for you, or maybe it's a reminder. In my life, it has proved true over and over again, and it was perhaps clearest in my life during this period. Had I not pushed myself into the unknown, I would have never had these opportunities. Had Guillaume not done the same, we would have never met and this story would not exist.

SUBCONTRACTING AND SETTING UP SHOP

GUILLAUME

With our combined knowledge and skills, Cole and I were able to move fast from the start, setting a strong foundation for GREEN CREATIVE. By the time Cole came back from his Thanksgiving trip at the end of 2010, we had many pieces of the puzzle already in place. We knew our product. We knew our market. We even had a clear division of roles. But we were still missing one crucial piece: a supplier.

By this point, we had already decided to position ourselves as the "manufacturer" among the many layers of the lighting industry. To do that, we needed to work with a supplier who had a factory to actually make the products.

When you're a startup, you need those few who'll take a chance on you—investors, employees, customers, and, in our case, suppliers. Anything we didn't do ourselves would need to be subcontracted out, and then our subcontractors would subcontract parts of their process out to other vendors.

Most car companies also work this way. They subcontract with various vendors and essentially work as integrators to assemble a finished product. The big difference is that car brands all find a way to look different. At lighting shows, a lot of the products look similar because everyone used the same general tooling, even if the inside of the product changed significantly depending on the supplier. We hoped to find a supplier that not only had all the tooling, but also one that had mastered the electronics, did their own testing, and had their own certification. We wanted to grow with a supplier and do as much of the work in-house as possible.

Of course, we couldn't simply click our fingers and make the perfect supplier appear. All the suppliers around us already worked with companies making hundreds of millions of dollars in revenue each year. They had little to gain from talking to us, especially since the most we could invest for an initial order was $20,000. That was chump change to them.

———

Part of finding the right supplier is dealing with the sheer number of them in China. Each of the vendors at the exhibition we went to before quitting our jobs was a potential supplier, and there were hundreds of them. We needed to narrow down our options. Thankfully, with some inside knowledge, I knew enough to begin the process.

First, I looked at which factories heavily invested in tooling. Those that did little in that department couldn't create products to the standard we wanted to achieve. We also needed a partner that could produce high-quality products and understand US requirements—both how to work with 110 volts and how to receive a UL and Energy Star certification. This final requirement was no small task as the US has a uniquely expensive certification process compared to a similar process somewhere like Europe.

With those requirements in mind, we were able to narrow down our potential factories from hundreds to just a few.

───────

As we began to visit the factories on our short list, the owners were shocked. Most of their clients were old, heavyset white men who flew to the factories once every year or two for a routine site visit before returning to the US. We were the polar opposite: two Mandarin-speaking men in their late twenties who drove their own cars. Many foreigners at the time had drivers, and it was unique for us to both have our own cars and Chinese driver's license.

To secure the supplier, we had to have a strong pitch. This is a place where Cole's expertise really came into play. We visited vendors as potential customers, but for us, it was way more important to make a good impression, as we were nobody, with no history, no funding besides our savings, and no business except the one in our heads. So, besides showing interest in them, we asked technical questions on manufacturing parts, tooling, and certification, which showed that, even though we had no business yet, we knew what we were talking about. Asking about MOQ (minimum order quantities) on tooling, customizing the product, and how to do it were questions they wouldn't get except from the likes of big OEMs (original equipment manufacturers) such as Philips or others. These visits were a stressful but fun experience.

Once we had our foot in the door, my experience within lighting factories would often get the managers on our side. I asked the right questions to let them know I understood things like optical design with different lenses, LED types, and even the electronic drivers used for dimming. Several suppliers were also interested in how closely Cole could position himself to key customers in the US. These conversations allowed us to appear like we knew what we were doing—even if we still had virtually no business to speak of.

With our combined work, we proved that if there was going to be a new player that would win some market share, it was going to be us. We were the proverbial horse to bet on.

At the same time, we were also interviewing each supplier. We considered price and performance, long-term R&D capabilities, and track record.

Finally, after what felt like endless meetings, we identified *the* supplier we wanted to work with. They were a producer for some of the big players in the space, including Philips, and they happened to believe that LED was the future and wanted to invest in that space. They'd even gone to the major players and explained that they had the factory ready to go, but no one else was ready to commit and invest in completely new engineering, tooling, and R&D.

We were.

While other companies didn't see the opportunity, we did, especially with a supplier that could move with speed. Most lighting players with standard setups were still subcontracting out work related to electronics, quality, and packaging. A new product would have to be validated by R&D in another country while the packaging was designed somewhere else. This process could take anywhere from six to nine months. That kind of timeline just doesn't make sense when the lifetime of a lighting product is only 12 to 18 months, but if we could keep almost everything in-house with this supplier, we could zoom past the competition. While other companies were finally getting around to launching a new product, we could be working on the next generation.

So we implored the supplier to give us a chance, and they told us to come and visit. The following week, we trekked out on a three-hour drive through the vast factories and farms sprinkled across Zhejiang, which neighbors Shanghai. We tucked in our collared shirts before we walked into the factory to look as professional as possible. After taking a tour, we sat down with the two managers, opened our laptops, and showed them our business plan. All we had was a basic PowerPoint that explained how we were going to dominate the LED lighting industry.

To our surprise, they believed in us, so much so that they were extremely accommodating with our first order. First, no minimum quantities. On top of this, they told us we could customize the products and the packaging— all because we treated them with respect and presented a vision worth believing in.

We had our supplier, and we dove right in, customizing four items for what would be Gen 1 of our product line. Altogether, the items would amount to ten SKUs (stock keeping units) because of various light colors and beam angles. It wasn't much, but it was a start.

Most importantly, we developed a key relationship. We would literally build our brand on the products we

BUILD RELATIONSHIPS, AND YOU'LL GET THE BACKSTAGE PASS

We didn't look at our supplier as a tool but as an equal. Because we built such a close relationship with them, we also had access to their resources. We got to see their R&D lab and knew what products were coming down their pipeline. Had we only visited the factory once a year, we'd have missed out on so much knowledge and technology. Even if some of the products or areas of the factory weren't relevant, we stayed curious, and our curiosity won us competitive intelligence. Moving fast was, of course, mutually beneficial; the supplier could access the market more quickly, and we could stay on the cutting edge of technology.

Simple kindness also went a long way. In China, companies are hierarchical. The CEO is on top, then midlevel managers, and then account/sales managers who are in charge of your specific account. It was easy enough to treat the people at the top well, but when we got sales/account managers on our side, they really fought on our behalf. Later down the line, they were willing to work their asses off to get our product through the manufacturing line on time.

made and developed within our supplier's factory. It was a relationship that would need to last for years to come, and it became just that. Years later, I even ended up being the best man at one of the sales managers' wedding. Ultimately, we ended up working with 12 suppliers, with three of four making up 90 percent of our supplies, but our original supplier was the only one that believed in us fully from the start. They placed a lot of trust in us, and we felt a real responsibility to prove to them that we could do what we said we were going to do.

———

With our subcontractors in place, we were nearly ready for 2011, but more still had to be done before the end of the year. I'd do whatever it took. I spent the last moments of 2010 stuck in a small hotel room at a coffee table, while on holiday with my family in Florida, finalizing our website so it'd be ready by 2011.

For our first year in business, we knew we'd need to share our message and provide potential customers with information. Since we didn't have any shop or storefront, a website was our way to let others know we were "live." Unfortunately, we couldn't get the domain name *greencreative.com*, so we settled for *green-creative.com*. Later, we were able to buy the exact domain, but at the time we knew we simply needed a site, whether it was called "green lighting," "great lighting," or just "plain old lighting."

Getting a domain name was only the first step. To build a website, we needed someone with design experience. Thankfully, our friend Malcolm from the UK, an incredibly talented designer who held a senior position at a design agency, offered to help us put together a well-designed site with a great user experience. When Cole found him, he was looking to make some extra money on the side. He not only helped us with our site, but he also helped us a ton further down the line once we had designers on board.

Most other websites in our industry were complicated to navigate. Potential customers emphasized how the Philips and GE websites were far from user-friendly. This told us exactly what not to do. When building our site, we took our time making sure visitors could easily reach each page, access necessary information about each product, and download further information about the products. This was important because we couldn't simply show our products. Since the technology was so new, we had to educate potential customers, and over time, we'd come to understand just how important this "LEDucation" section was.

But none of that would matter or come to pass if I didn't get the website live for 2011. I knew Cole was sitting on his hands, waiting to be able to show customers more. In the end, all the up-front effort paid off.

It's easy to underestimate the time needed to make a quality website. When you're just starting out, you don't have any copy, images, or navigation. But when you invest that up-front time to build a quality site, you won't have to think about it nearly as much moving forward. Even when you do need to add a new web page, you'll have a template to work from and know how to construct each page. We kept the same site for five years and drew thousands of monthly visitors for many of the primary keywords we targeted.

IN SAN FRANCISCO IT WAS HUSTLE OR DIE

COLE

On December 31 of 2010, Guillaume and I kept our promises and quit our jobs. We'd gone full-time with our business. We had a supplier in place and were on our way to producing Gen 1 of our product. What we didn't have, however, were customers or distribution channel partners.

It was time for me to head to the US.

We said our goodbyes and I made my way to Shanghai Pudong International Airport. I'll never forget the feeling of stepping onto that plane in Shanghai. I'd lived there for four years and was venturing into the unknown.

A couple of hours into the flight, the steward announced that it was midnight in Shanghai. A new year. It felt fitting. Before I dozed off for some much-needed sleep, a couple of lines repeated in my mind. I thought back to their origin— one of my favorite graduation speeches ever, in which Baz Luhrmann puts an essay to a song in "Everybody's Free (to Wear Sunscreen)." He says you should live in New York but leave before it makes you too hard and that you should live in Northern California but leave before it makes you too soft. Now here I was, on my way to San Francisco.

When the plane hit the tarmac at SFO, the race was on. It was hustle or die. There was just one issue: I was trying to presell a product we didn't yet have. But even then, San Francisco felt right, and not just because I liked the Baz Luhrmann song. It felt right because it seemed like the ideal hub for GREEN CREATIVE. I was finally there— Silicon Valley. Just being there made us feel like we were a tech company.

In preparation for the move, I Googled like a maniac. *Who buys lighting? Who buys light bulbs?* I formed a master list of anyone I could call and started calling some of the names on the list while still in China. I stayed up late with the hope of reaching someone. If I did, I'd give them my little pitch and try to set up a time to meet after the move.

By the point I started making these calls, I already had some practice with making our business look larger than it was. Guillaume had spoken with dozens of factory owners and had to convince all of them—one way or another—that we were legitimate. Now, on the phone, I had to come up with some new tactics.

When the person on the other end of the line asked a question, I'd say, "Let me check with my boss." I then went and checked in with myself, literally, stalling long enough to figure out how to respond. Thankfully, most of the calls stayed surface level, and I didn't need to get into details about our products or organization. The goal was simple: set a time to get in front of someone.

By the time I landed in San Francisco, I had a handful of meetings set up. Unfortunately, most of these "potential customers" were tiny mom-and-pop shops. I wasn't fooling myself; I knew we'd never do enough volume with them. Still, I had to try, if only for the sake of practice.

In my mind, I held on to simple logic: *turn over enough stones, and eventually I'll find the right people.*

ALL THE
LITTLE DETAILS

GUILLAUME

While Cole hopped around San Francisco in search of our first customer, I was back in China figuring out all the little details. It was one thing to have a supplier, but it was another to get everything right with our first products.

Thankfully, our supplier had an LED product line they'd already developed, with the right certification and all. We could leverage what they already had and simply customize the product to fit our needs. It was a perfect scenario.

Unfortunately, the certification got a little tricky. UL has a number next to the UL logo, and if someone is motivated enough, they can look to see where the product came from. We didn't want anyone tracking the number back to the supplier, so we spent a large sum and I put in hours of paperwork just to make sure the UL and Energy Star were linked to GREEN CREATIVE.

The Energy Star certification was particularly important. Energy Star is a US government certification that states your product is eco-friendly. It allows companies and end users to get rebates from utility companies. It was a key part of our business and a general market requirement.

Getting Energy Star certification is a long and expensive process for R&D. They test 40 pieces of a product line for 6,000 to 10,000 hours. Every 1,000 hours, they test the product's light output, quality of light, and color rendering. Over the years, every time we created a new product, we had to test it for six to ten months before we could get that key certification.

After it's tested, Energy Star continues to follow up. They'll pick up products on the market and test them to make sure they're the same products that you gave them for testing. The good news is that the products remain Energy Star certified until there's a problem.

Unfortunately, a few years down the line, we faced one of our biggest challenges yet when we lost our Energy Star certification.

As part of the continued certification, they require a report on the volume of sales for each product they've certified. In 2013, we missed one of the deadlines for sending in the report. When that happened, we got a letter notifying us that *all* our products were pulled from Energy Star. We never got a warning notice, simply a statement saying we were kicked out.

On the sales side, our existing business was damaged because we had unnecessary headaches from our product. The future of the business was hurt too; potential customers who looked at specs and details were unsure whether our products were Energy Star certified.

Our customers installing our products couldn't find them on the Energy Star website. Others' rebates were rejected.

We did our best to explain why we lost the certification and how we were working to get it back. It should've been as simple as telling everyone we had Energy Star certification and moving on, but it wasn't. All we could do was focus on the solution.

We called all our customers and got ahead of the issue. After apologizing, we explained the situation and promised to keep them in the loop. We let them know when we'd get the certification again. We were helpful and accommodating. If people had stock that no longer qualified, we took it back. If a rebate didn't kick in, we offered to pay the difference. We made it clear that we had our customers' backs.

Because rebates typically happen at the state level, we petitioned individual states to give our product an exception. We got approvals for Washington and California. From there, we informed the customers that our products still qualified in those regions.

We also focused our efforts on contacting Energy Star to get our certification back. We sent them reports and reference letters from key people in the industry in hopes of speeding up the process. Thankfully, we had a good working relationship with them. They knew we were at the edge of new lighting technology and provided top-line products, so they always wanted to learn from us. However, because they're a government entity, we couldn't stop them from kicking us out.

Losing the Energy Star certification was a huge obstacle for our company and our growth, but it taught us a lot.

We got to practice our motto and see it work. Ninety-five percent of our energy needed to be focused on the solution, not the problem itself. What little time we spent on the problem was simply to ensure it didn't happen again.

Moving forward, we used our own laboratory for optimizing and validating all samples or prototypes prior to certification. Even when tooling wasn't ready, we worked on expensive prototyping projects so that the performance testing could get started ahead of time.

We also learned that it was easy to tell customers what they wanted to hear and promise to be a good business partner, but truthfully, it wasn't until that relationship was tested that the customer could truly trust that we had their back. Many companies show their true colors during a crisis, focusing more on pointing fingers and panicking than on showing up for their customers and partners. We learned the importance of taking care of people during adversity.

Finally, we learned how important it was to keep supporting each other. Cole supported me through the whole process. Rather than pointing fingers, he worked on solving the business side of problems. We were on the same team. It wouldn't make sense for us to shout at each other every time something went wrong. I already knew that I'd messed up. All we could do was work together and find solutions.

But having Energy Star, otherwise, was always a boon. Going back to 2011, Cole realized that certain utility rebates for LEDs would fund entire building retrofits. He'd have to submit all the paperwork with project details, photos of the spot, and verification of how many lamps were needed. The overall process was tedious but worth it.

We used this rebate successfully with our first big sale and later leveraged it often with distributors and end users. After all, people were much more willing to use a $40 light bulb if they could get a full rebate for it. In some parts of the country, end users would only get partial rebates, but we still made sure to educate them about this benefit. Rebates became such a large part of the business that we eventually had an employee completely dedicated to them.

But once we had Energy Star certification for our first product, my next goal was to set up inspection and testing for quality and performance. Thankfully, I had another connection I could lean on—my former colleague Matthieu.

He was in charge of manufacturing and quality control (QC) and also involved in R&D. He had a very strong personality that you had to handle with care, but there were very positive results if you were able to accommodate him. He understood lab and inspection requirements and expressed his desire to be involved. He offered his support and provided much-needed insight.

From the start, I wanted to be extremely transparent about our inspection and the standards we hit. It would play in our favor and add to our credibility. We needed to show we weren't random guys with a pipe dream. We needed a real inspection process that included testing the temperature of the product and the light performance and a review of the key interior components. As I set this up with the factory manager, I realized how extensive the process was. Every detail needed to be checked several times before our product could be shipped and sold.

Finally, after several iterations and a lot of testing, we had our Gen 1. Seeing our products with all our specifications, color finishes, and logo almost brought me to tears. You can touch the products, test them, and finalize everything, but when you see the final customized version, it's a whole different feeling. Our baby was born and finally took its first breath.

We placed our first order for just a few hundred pieces of each item, a total of 2,500 pieces. At the time, it felt like an enormous feat, but in the grand scheme of things, it was a tiny order (less than 10 percent of the size of the supplier's average order).

I was finally able to bring Cole a demo case, which was essentially a suitcase he could take to potential customers. They could see the product firsthand. We'd already put up a simple website, but now we could add more information about the product and the space. We shared articles about LED power, technology, and the ROI (return on investment), which drew new traffic to the site. We even had a digital catalog we could send interested parties by email, creating further legitimacy.

With all these details in place and a product in hand, I felt like we'd truly accomplished something. We'd put in the up-front work, and we had something tangible to show for it. We just had to sell something.

ALL THE NOES
BEFORE A YES

COLE

A few weeks after I landed in San Francisco, Guillaume came to visit to scope out the city with me. I picked him up at the train station at 11 at night. He was stunned. He wasn't used to seeing so much trash or so many people on drugs. We were used to China, where everything appeared clean and safe. For him, this was a whole new world.

For several days, we took our new, beautiful display box around the city to show prospective customers. The suitcase was so heavy that we had to take turns lugging it.

By the end of the trip, Guillaume ended up with a stress fracture in his foot from all the weight.

While a few people graciously listened to our spiel, no one took the bait. One person spent hours asking thorough questions only to say he was thinking about investing $5,000 into the business. We were dejected by this amount, and then only a few days later, he followed up with a less-than-ideal message. He thought we weren't going to be successful. So that one didn't work out.

But we didn't pay much attention to the noes. We'd been working away in our apartment in Shanghai for six months, and everything had been theoretical up to this point. Even with rejection after rejection, we were just excited to meet with people and share what we'd created. With our visit list done, and no yeses to be had, in one final attempt, we tried to pitch a furniture store across from our hotel. Sure enough, it was a no from them.

After Guillaume left, I continued to meet with more people in San Francisco. I still hit brick wall after brick wall. I couldn't figure it out, but soon enough I found out why.

We'd based our first product on what our supplier already had. It was essentially off the shelf and not even close to the best in the market. Worse than that, the first generation of what we made was significantly inferior to what was coming onto the market.

Additionally, everyone was comparing us to Lighting Science, the main LED company in the US. The company had a ton of funding and naturally had a superior product, better packaging, and better marketing. They had products in Home Depot and made millions in revenue per year. Then there was us. We had a few thousand dollars in a savings account.

Thankfully, I'd been in sales long enough to know how to position a product as something for the future. Even our first-gen model was 90 percent more efficient than existing halogen and incandescent lighting and would last 50 times longer. LED lights are the low-hanging fruit of energy savings. If you can screw out a halogen bulb and screw in an LED, you can save 90 percent in energy immediately. Lights use 20 percent of the power on the grid, so if you can reduce 20 percent of the overall energy by 90 percent, you can really create massive energy savings.

More importantly, I could fully stand behind the product. Of the eight billion light sockets in the US, few had LEDs in them. If we could be part of converting these lights, we could prevent 15 power plants from needing to be built, which would be the equivalent of taking millions of cars off the road for a year. I knew there was a higher purpose to what we were doing, and it showed each time I presented the product.

Unfortunately, not many end users or distributors were as dedicated to the mission as we were. Getting a yes from someone would take a little more convincing. LED lights had been in the US for a few years, but they were terrible in quality and very expensive. A lot of people tried selling them, but because their quality was suspect, many early adopters were extremely underwhelmed by the technology. Additionally, most of the big players discouraged LED because they were happy selling halogen and fluorescent products. Entering the market would be an uphill climb.

I decided to use some of my time cold-calling lighting distributors across the US, doing my best to convince them to buy our product.

Unfortunately, this was a chicken-and-egg situation. No one wants to sell your product unless they have a reason to sell your product. And for them to have a reason, other people need to be selling it. Our biggest pushback was the fact that people hadn't heard of GREEN CREATIVE. People would ask, "What if we buy your product, and the life of the company doesn't outlast the warranty?" That was a fair point. I didn't blame them. We had little to show that we weren't making thrown-together products that might burn down their building.

I kept pounding the pavement in search of a sale as the deadline for our products arriving at my doorstep crept closer and closer with still no buyers. The pressure mounted. I considered the fact that lights are a technology product, much like a cell phone. Sure, some people might still buy it a year later, but the selling price would decrease significantly over time. In the LED world, that looked like a 15 percent annual decrease. Given that the technology was improving so much every year, if we couldn't sell our products quickly, they'd be obsolete, and we'd be forced to write them off as a loss.

We were entrepreneurs with a product no one wanted to buy. We weren't the first to be in this position, and we won't be the last. There was no choice but to keep going.

———

One day, while hopping from store to store, a distributor's truck passed me on the street. I dropped the coffee in my hand and made chase. I was more than desperate. My feet flew over the cement for two blocks until I caught the driver at a red light. I ran up to the driver's-side door. "Who sells your lights?" I spat out, still catching my breath. "I'd love to speak to someone from your company."

"Oh, you should talk to Dan," the driver replied.

He gave me Dan's full name. I jotted it and the distributor's name down as fast as I could. The guys in the truck looked at me like I was crazy.

I may have been.

Dan turned out to be a salesman who directly serviced the San Francisco market. I found his number in the company directory and gave him a call.

Then another.

And another. This time he picked up and, with a bit of convincing, he agreed to meet me at my office. I'd annoyed him to the point of no return, and he wanted to check out our office to see if we were legit.

This presented a dilemma. GREEN CREATIVE didn't have an office, and it would be difficult to meet at an office that didn't exist. I had to think fast. Somehow I found a shared office space, which wasn't particularly common at the time. I told the space's manager that I potentially wanted to use it as a long-term office and asked for a free hour. He agreed.

I met with Dan at the shared space. We had an hour before we'd be kicked out or I'd be charged for the time. I hustled to keep the meeting under an hour and then strong-armed Dan into having lunch with me so we could continue our conversation. When I asked him to pay for his portion of the meal (since I was broke), he remarked that it was the first time a potential partner ever forced him to pay for his own lunch. It became a joke for every subsequent meeting.

After all the talking, Dan finally looked at me and said, "Sorry, it's not gonna happen."

He was used to being wined and dined by people from billion-dollar corporations, and here was this 25-year-old guy in a knockoff WeWork, clearly with no money and no real business, trying to convince him to use our products. So, while I understood, the words landed hard. How much more could I do? How many more vans would I need to chase?

———

The next week, I took things up a notch. If I couldn't get a distributor to say yes, maybe I could convince a contractor. After all, distributors sold product to contractors, so why couldn't I sell directly to them?

That week, each morning, I woke up early and headed to a contractor's office to wait for someone to open the front door. I'd sneak in before it closed, and then I'd get to looking for someone to approach—anyone who looked like they might possibly be interested in buying lights. And for me, that was just about anyone.

I was amazed when, finally, one of the contractors communicated an interest in the product. However, my hopes were quickly dashed when he asked to sample the product in a space. I didn't have products for him to sample. All I had was my little briefcase, and that wasn't going to cut it.

———

During this same time, I also decided to go after engineers for some of the largest buildings in downtown San Francisco. These were end users. Engineers were the ones

who actually procured and installed lights in their buildings. They're a tight-knit group who are not particularly
welcoming to outsiders. They'd arrive early, sometimes
as early as 4:00 a.m., to assess their buildings and make
any needed repairs before people arrived. If there was
nothing to do, they'd usually drink coffee and read the
paper. It was kind of a quiet time for them. They had their
routine, and that routine didn't usually involve someone
sneaking in to try to sell them products.

I set my alarm clock an hour earlier and headed to a
different downtown building each day. Sleep was something I was more than willing to sacrifice. I was determined to catch someone as they arrived in the morning.
I stood next to the garage door, and when an engineer
drove their car into the garage, I'd sneak in behind them
on foot. I'd wait a few minutes for the engineer to get settled into their office—just enough time for them to grab
their coffee and newspaper—and then I'd knock on their
door and immediately start selling.

To sustain these early morning visits, I had to get creative with my budget once I started traveling to other cities in and around the Bay Area. I figured if I could get
up early and meet building engineers in the Bay, I could

do the same thing in surrounding cities. Soon enough, I found a routine that worked. Upon arriving at each new city, I found an In-N-Out Burger for my go-to meal, and I used their restroom to brush my teeth and wash my face.

Instead of a hotel, I parked in a residential area. Even if I could afford a hotel, I saw little point in it. I'd only be there for a few hours. My technique was the better, and cheaper, option. So I cozied up in my car, hung up my clothes strategically so people couldn't see inside, and slept in the back. The next day, I woke early, found an inexpensive gym, and paid the $15 day fee so that I could use their showers, shave, and then get ready for the day. From there, I began selling.

Most were less than enthused to see me. People would say, "This is a Philips building" or "This is a GE building." They all had brand affiliations, but I was relentless. One opening we were able to take advantage of was that big brands like GE and Philips were really stingy with providing samples, engineers wanted to try before they bought, and once we had samples available, we were more than willing to share, which ended up giving us a lot of our initial business.

But I couldn't let their reactions dampen my enthusiasm. I had to stay motivated to get over our first major hump and sell something. And sure enough, I finally did. Two of the engineers were so annoyed with me that they finally caved. They didn't care about our brand but were interested in LED lights, so they preordered a couple hundred lights each. It wasn't much, but it was a start.

———

I kept at it like this for weeks, and by March 1, I'd presold about 30 percent of the lights. This was great, but I had to sell the rest. I was ready to try anything. I looked for any creative avenue I could take. From my research, I found an LED show in Santa Clara that seemed like it could be a perfect opportunity to display our fancy new demo cases to potential customers. The problem? It cost $20,000 to display your products and required a $5,000 deposit. Without thinking about it, I put the deposit down, hoping this would be our winning ticket. It wasn't.

If I had slowed down for a moment, I would've realized that there wouldn't be any customers at a manufacturing show. It was a show for suppliers curious about new LED parts, not finished products.

I tried to fix the mistake, writing several emails saying that we were sick and couldn't make it or that my grandfather had died. Alas, it was truly nonrefundable. We ate that cost.

Unfortunately, there was no turning back. Even though the LED show was a failure that wasn't even worth showing up to, I knew I simply had to keep moving. I knew that, at the end of the day, sales is a numbers game, no matter how difficult a product is to sell. I kept walking into furniture stores, hotels, and restaurants. I was going to make this work.

In almost every conversation, Lighting Science would again pop up. I'd finish my sales pitch, and they'd ask me if I'd ever heard of Lighting Science. I'd tell them that of course I had, at which point they'd so kindly point out that their products were better than ours.

Lighting Science had recently come out with the first major LED products in the US. When they were first released, it was the equivalent of the iPhone coming out, only in the LED world. They were the company with the most money to spend on R&D, focusing solely on the LED lamp. They had a heavy VC firm behind them, and their product had a year-and-a-half lead on the rest of the market. They were sleek and clean and used a specific construction using aluminum housing that would later become an industry standard. Everyone else's lights—including ours—looked like they were from the space age. But people didn't want lights that looked like what technology was going to be; they just wanted nice-looking lights.

Lighting Science could also replace almost any other light, one-for-one. So, naturally, people were comparing us to them. Could we do the same? The answer was no.

Interestingly enough, Lighting Science would end up having too much demand and not enough supply to keep up. They hadn't taken steps to set up proper manufacturing or subcontracting, and that mistake cost them in the end. Customers could only wait so long for a product to arrive.

On the other hand, we didn't have nearly *enough* customers to buy our small shipment of product. By the middle of March, we were six weeks out from delivery. The lights had begun their long journey across the seas, and I was still floundering, wondering how we were going to make this business a reality. Every day we didn't make a sale was a day closer to the product arriving. We needed to find a home to prove that this business would be successful.

Unless something changed, come April, I'd have a lot of unsold product on my hands. Then it hit me. It was actually worse than that—I had no place to store it all!

I quickly reached out to a few 3PL (third-party logistics) warehouses that did fulfillment, but they charged too much for our budget, which was essentially zero. I'd have to go a different, more creative route.

When I first arrived in San Francisco, I noticed the "$1 for Month 1" signs at storage facilities all over the place.

Perfect solution.

I found a storage facility on Toland Street in downtown San Francisco. The deal was $1 for the first month of storage and then $80 per month after that. Eighty dollars was too much. I'd have to have a lot of first months.

I reserved the first month under my name. After that first month, I used Guillaume's, followed by my dad's, my mom's, and even my sister's name to continually get that promotion price. This meant switching the storage spaces each month. Even though we only had a few pallets of product, it was a lot for one person and would take a full day at the end of each month to cart the lights from one space to the next. The effort was worth the savings, though. That couple hundred dollars saved went a long way.

———

In the coming months, these storage facilities would be our fulfillment centers. I'd call customers in the morning and walk the streets of San Francisco in the afternoons. When I'd finally manage to secure an order, I'd head to our "fulfillment center" and load the lights into my car to make the delivery or head to FedEx to mail out a sample.

The one-dollar first month was not the only way I made things work with our budget in the beginning. I found every corner I could cut. I had about $20,000 to live on; I couldn't afford an actual apartment. I found sublets through Craigslist, did a lot of couch surfing with strangers, and spent a few nights in my little Mazda3, which my grandfather had kindly bought for me back in 2011 when I first moved back to the US.

I'd buy four-dollar burritos or sustain myself with peanut butter and bread. Whenever Guillaume came to visit, the policies didn't change. I greeted him with a luxurious four-dollar burrito and an inflatable mattress that we returned when he left, along with blankets and pillows.

But, finally, I decided I'd had enough. It was time to get a real lease. With the little money we had, we were able to afford a former crack house in the middle of San Francisco that came in at a crisp $600. Shortly after moving in, the owner told me his friend was going to crash on the couch. *Great*, I thought.

His friend had served 17 years in jail for dealing crack. We didn't get along very well, but thankfully I was hardly in the apartment. I asked the landlord to at least find a place for him to stay when Guillaume visited, but it turned out that the guy would otherwise be sleeping on the streets. I'm not sure where he went, but one time after Guillaume left, the guy came back and got in my face in such a way that I thought I was going to die. After that, I was on edge.

A week later, I walked into the apartment. My closet door was open. I was convinced someone was inside and called the police. They showed up. They drew their guns, and I followed them as they walked into the house. I imagined people inside who wanted to hurt me. I was terrified and started wondering what the hell was I doing living like this. Nobody was there. The cops were just as relieved as I was.

ALWAYS IN LEAN MODE

GUILLAUME

Throughout the first year of business, we saw ourselves like a speedboat among ocean liners. Being the small, unknown player in the market came with challenges and perks. We had to hustle on every front, but we were able to move quickly and think fast.

I spent about a third of my time in the US. It was fun to hear Cole's creative ways of stretching the budget, and I always had my own stories to share. When I visited suppliers, for example, I often stayed in $15 hotels that were so disgusting, I'd sleep fully dressed. I never dared to get under the sheets. Inevitably, the supplier would send someone to pick me up from my hotel, and I'd have to tell them to pick me up at a nice hotel down the road. I'd walk or take a cab to the other hotel in the morning to appear as if I'd stayed there the night before. A little "fake it till you make it" seemed to be working for us both.

When we started the company, I didn't want to work from home, so I shared an office the size of a small bedroom with two friends who ran their own company. At $200 a month, the price to rent my portion of the space was perfect, but it wasn't such a perfect place for meetings. When someone suggested we meet in my office, I quickly suggested we meet at a coffee shop or hotel lobby instead. For the entire first three years in business, even as my team in China grew to four, we all crammed into this tiny space and managed to have less than a handful of visitors ever see our "office."

Still, I could only cut so many corners in China. For credibility, we at least needed to be able to show that we had an active company. The problem was that I had no money to make that happen. I couldn't even hire an accountant. The $1,500 a month we'd need for that was certainly not in the budget. Thankfully, Cole had already set up QuickBooks, which gave us some idea of sales. But months after our initial order, we still had little idea of how our money looked. All we knew was that any money that came in would need to go straight back into the business.

———

When I worked in trading, I only had to pay attention to a couple of costs. When I later worked at a factory, I got my first taste of how complex costing could get once you started to include sourcing, production, quality, and packaging costs. Once we started our business, I thought I knew what to expect, but there were still more costs to add, including shipping and inventory.

In any business, the cost is a combination of costs plus margins. In our case, four key components represented the majority of the cost in our BOM (bill of material), which gives the full set of components of a given product. From the earliest stage, we required a BOM-level cost communication with vendors. While not always fully accurate, this gave us an idea of the manufacturer's margin structure and our product component cost breakdown so we could focus on the essential items. This kind of BOM cost and communication also opened the door for improvement or product change later on.

Every year, the components improved dramatically. It was the equivalent of how the iPhone goes from one generation to the next. For us to stay ahead of the market, we had to break down each individual component of the product. We didn't just take the word of the factory that they had better components. We wanted to interact directly and be part of the negotiation and decision-making around which components we'd use in our products.

To track costs, I created a costing sheet based on my previous work experience. We included all the costs in our process. If the finished product was quoted at $20, $5 was the LEDs, $3 was the lens, $3 was the heatsink, $3 was driver electronics, $3 was assembly, and the remaining $3 was the margin. And this isn't even accounting for other certification investments. In the end, costing became our savior in growing profitably. Because we knew how much was coming out at each turn, I knew what we'd be left with in the end for margin.

Even when we later added a more robust accounting system, we still relied on our simple Excel costing sheet because of how effective it was. I ultimately handed it to our new general manager, Bertrand, like a sacred item passed down.

> Many businesses don't keep track of costing at every level. Because this is the case, they assume a lot about how much they're spending. This is a critical error. Knowing your exact costs will not only allow you to have a clear sense of how your business functions but will also ultimately allow you to set pricing correctly.

Down the line, even when we started to experience more success, we didn't think it was time to live like kings. We still worked around the clock, and weekends were for commissions and accounting. Working six days per week was the norm, and we still cut costs when possible.

Whenever I'd fly to the US, I wouldn't choose direct flights because they were too expensive. I'd save a couple hundred dollars by choosing connecting flights, and that was worth it for us. One time, I went through LA en route to San Francisco. Due to a delay, I couldn't leave until the next morning. Since hotels were too expensive, I had to find a spot in the terminal, which was open all night. Eventually, I decided to sleep on a bench at a McDonald's. I woke up early, bought an Egg McMuffin, and caught my flight out.

These kinds of situations were the norm for us. We played at the edge, knowing that each dollar counted.

We couldn't always relate to the venture-funded businesses around us. These companies started with money and scaled up the organization with employee infrastructure and other costs, hoping that the investment turned into sales for the business.

Our model looked nothing like that. Since starting GREEN CREATIVE at the end of 2010, we had to simply keep taking steps, even if they weren't in the "right" order. We were the very definition of all in.

GETTING TO THE END USER AND OUR FIRST BIG SALE

COLE

With so much of the shipment still sitting in storage, I decided it was time to simply walk the streets of San Francisco and go door-to-door. I'd never lost a job while selling someone else's product, and I wasn't going to lose our business because I couldn't make sales. So I set out with my ambition and a suitcase of lights.

Whenever I entered a coffee shop, restaurant, bar, or hotel, I asked if they had an outlet I could borrow. Assuming I was looking for somewhere to charge my phone, they'd gesture toward an available plug-in. I'd thank them, head over to the outlet, and set up our box of prototypes. Once I had the box plugged in and the products on display, I'd call the employee back over.

I was usually met with confusion. But before that could overtake the moment, I'd launch into my presentation. Without fail, they'd respond, "I don't decide what lights we use, so I can't really help you."

Soon enough, I realized the reason for their objection. When a light bulb goes out at a McDonald's, the employee puts in an order for a new light. Then a third-party vendor will service their store, using supplies from one of their many warehouses to replace the light bulb. The vendor wants to make sure they maintain uniformity and are using lights they know work, so they work directly with distributors for their orders.

In the majority of my sales pitches thus far, with the exception of the occasional mom-and-pop shops, the end users would often refer me back to the distributor they worked with. Clearly, we needed to find a way to partner with a distributor if we wanted to make real progress.

By June, I'd heard that a distributor had started to warm up to us. However, it might be more accurate to say

TO GROW A BUSINESS EFFECTIVELY, YOU MUST KNOW WHOM TO SELL TO, AND WHEN

One of the benefits of selling to end users would be that we'd have a higher margin. We wouldn't need to sell as many products to produce the same amount of revenue. However, selling through distributors would give us scale.

We began with the end user. We convinced them to buy LED products, and then we convinced them to buy our LED products. We knew this approach would eventually help us get distribution involved.

If we threatened the business of distributors, they'd have to carry our line. If enough end users asked for our products, distributors eventually wouldn't have a choice.

A go-to-market strategy is different from a long-term strategy. As we grew over the years, we decided to protect distribution and not go direct at all. We made sure that distributors were aware that distribution wasn't just our primary channel; it was our only channel.

Every approach has its own pain and gain. However, we chose the one with more initial pain but longer-term gain by going through distribution in the end.

we'd started to annoy them. After all, I was calling all their local accounts, and they likely felt threatened by this, concerned that I'd try to sell around them. I was unwilling to take no for an answer, and if a distributor wasn't going to sell our products, they'd have to deal with their customers buying our products directly from us. It was either ignore me and lose sales or work with me and we could get them together. I was confident we'd eventually be able to negotiate a deal with them, but they weren't biting yet.

Lighting distributors felt comfortable selling halogen and fluorescent bulbs, but they weren't nearly as interested in promoting LED lights, especially since they were still so expensive. Every month, a lighting distributor is used to getting the same replacement orders for the same lights they've been selling for decades. The last thing they wanted to do was sell an LED light, which had a much longer life span, which would increase the time between sales. It would be a larger sale—$50 to $70 instead of $3 to $5—but then they wouldn't see that socket again for the rest of their careers.

Because the distributors were resistant to selling LEDs, we had to blaze into the market and inform people about the groundbreaking technology of LED lights.

This was easier said than done. Most people didn't even know what LED lights were. Half of my sales work was selling the merits of LED lighting and why it was worthwhile. On top of that, I also had to try and sell our product.

The "LEDucation" section of our website helped by illustrating all the pros associated with switching to LED. The biggest thing we pushed was that you got the same lighting for a significantly lower wattage. Our lights had a significantly longer life span, but also, they consumed around 90 percent less energy—all while creating a better-looking building. You saved on electricity and had a product that lasted significantly longer, which meant you could spend less managing all the lights.

It was clear that LED lights would eventually win out as the primary lighting technology. But it wasn't so clear when distributors would consider LED or who'd be the most successful brand to weather the storm of this disruptive technology.

———

The first major win, and the real beginning of things in the US, finally came from selling lights to a furniture store in Chinatown. We'd first met them when Guillaume was visiting at the start of the year and we'd stayed for a week at the Grant Hotel, just across the street from their store. When we walked in, we were impressed by the immaculate furniture, art, and chandeliers for sale. More importantly, there were thousands of lights that illuminated their store. We couldn't help but salivate at the opportunity.

What stood out right away was the contrast between what was in the store and who was selling it. The salesmen called each other Marc and Lorenzo. They might've fooled some tourists, but I wasn't fooled. Being Jewish, I spotted their thick Israeli accents from a mile away.

These guys were funny, gregarious, and great at what they did. They worked their magic and sold a lot. But I was ready to work some magic of my own. Initially, they had little interest in hearing me out, but soon enough I convinced them to take a look at the ROI calculations— to see how much they could save on their electricity bill. After 90 days, the project would pay for itself, and then it would create huge savings over the next five years. It was a no-brainer that I finally got across by showing up every day until they made a decision.

But a decision they made!

Finally, after three months of bargaining, they handed us an order. It was our first order for thousands of lights. It depleted most of our inventory. We'd certainly remember this milestone for a long time. There was a demand for our product. It looked like this was going to work.

LEARNING THE MARKET ON THE MOVE

GUILLAUME

The lighting industry shifts quickly. If we wanted to win, we'd have to stay up to speed. By this point, we had a decent picture of how things worked. We understood that end users looked to distributors, and distributors worked with manufacturers on the production side and with manufacturer reps on the sales side. Still, we had a lot to learn about the market itself. What did the market want? What were people willing to buy? What should our next product line be?

To get answers, I'd fly from China to the US every six to eight weeks. While I was there, I'd visit customers, work with Cole, and research at retail and commercial distribution stores. I wanted to develop a clear understanding of what end users looked for and what drove distributors and installers to make their decisions.

To understand the market, I walked into stores like Home Depot or Lowe's and looked at everything they had on their shelves. It was one thing to see the product online. It was something completely different to see what was actually happening on the ground. A product available online might not even be on the sales floor, or if it was, it might be poorly positioned. The number of items on the shelves also gave a clearer idea of volume. When I looked at the shelf space for existing technology, such as incandescent, halogen, or CFL, I could also understand the overall volume and ensure our upcoming product pipeline made sense.

In a retail store, say a supermarket, the shelf space is based on two factors: margin and volume. If a similar product is repeated four to five times in width, it's because that product is selling. So, by looking at the shelf, I was able to understand what was moving and how. It gave me a visual interpretation of the market opportunity that hit my brain and turned on the "let's work on this *now*" action switch.

I bought any samples I could and loaded them into big, cheap suitcases from Ross. Each time I landed in Shanghai, I had two suitcases full of samples in tow. I was afraid of the issues I'd face if I was stopped. If I was, at the least it would've been a full day at the airport answering customs' questions. In China, customs was more concerned with things like import tax and certification. In the US, I did get stopped several times but simply explained I was carrying R&D samples and showed them a catalog. That was good enough for them.

When exiting the airport in China, I'd have to exit through customs, but I learned a trick. I could wait until they stopped checking 100 percent of the line, wait until the numbers died down, and then walk through as briskly as I could. There was often still an agent to spot-check, but I never ran into any major issue this way.

Each time I traveled, I'd also have to get out cash for the trip, and when I got back, I'd have to exchange the money again. Since the bank had a poor exchange rate, I'd regularly exchange large sums on the street in China. I'd see the old man who did the exchange sitting in front of the bank, and I'd walk up to him with my wad of cash. I didn't think anything of it. I needed the money to use, so I found a workaround. A lot of things were like that for us. We simply found a way.

It was no different when it came time to test other samples of other companies' products I had from the States. To do this, I hired Théo—an engineer from my previous company—to work part-time and help us out. I bought some testing equipment (a temperature measurement machine, some soldering equipment, and electrical sensors) and delivered it to his house. His wife was not so happy about this. Thankfully, my previous company soon allowed me to use their testing equipment at night and on weekends, so the home testing came to an end.

With the samples, we tried to reverse engineer the process and figure out how to meet the market with our next generation. In disassembling each item, we saw all the key components and construction. A single light bulb would go through the equivalent of a four-hour engineering check. We'd test for performance, light intensity, beam angle, and dimming.

After a lot of testing, we began to have an idea of where

we'd head next. One of the most superficial changes to make was to change our product to white because everyone complained that our first product's cover shell was black, and, over time, we became known as the company with the black lights, which actually helped differentiate us up front. When we got started, we didn't have R&D capabilities, access to LED components, or money to reach out at those levels, so we partnered with a vendor hand in hand. But when it came to Gen 2, we decided to implement all the feedback and launch them as white. As soon as we started to show people the color of the lights, we started to hear, "Why aren't they black? They should be black." People grew used to our product's color and were disappointed in the change. It was a good lesson. The customer would always push back, but if we felt strongly about a choice, we needed to stick with it. We stuck with white.

Most importantly, we knew we'd need to increase lighting performance significantly in our next generation— from 75 watts up to 90 watts or even 120 watts, depending on the light.

———

Listening to potential buyers and market feedback helped us define our target more properly. This is why trade shows and fairs, whether we were exhibitors or not, were very meaningful.

To discover new vendors and products, I attended two big trade shows each year—one in Guangzhou and one in Hong Kong—in addition to a third one that was smaller and more multi-industry. This was a huge part of my job. Cole and I both knew that some of the best products and improvements came from companies in China, especially smaller ones that innovated and created products at lower prices.

These shows were usually two to three days. They were intense. Held in enormous buildings, the spaces felt never-ending. I'd walk 20,000 steps a day and pick up any food I could find. I didn't want to miss a thing. I had to keep moving.

At these early shows, I fell into the trap of spending time with low-value-added people or factories. Some of the vendors from the show turned out to be putting on fronts without much to show in real life. There'd just be a table with a few samples, and then I'd visit a so-called factory to find nothing there. But I was used to this by now;

this was how "respect" worked in China. A person might show up in a fancy car or, in this case, hide behind a fancy booth, but it didn't necessarily mean a thing.

I, on the other hand, didn't always abide by the rule of having a fancy front. Because I had so many potential vendors to visit, I rented out the smallest car in China, called a QQ, a sort of ever so slightly elongated smart car (if you're familiar with them), and drove it all over Guangdong. When I'd show up in my mini car, I'd get a good laugh from the vendor. Thankfully, my Chinese helped me connect and continue the conversation, but other times, they simply couldn't take me seriously, and I had to move on.

———

As we expanded our network of vendors, we realized how invaluable they were. Not only do vendors manufacture the products, but also they understand the entire cost of production. Our manufacturing partners gave us inside knowledge of the industry. They knew which products were most relevant and which were in demand. Our partnerships with them allowed us to get started and stay ahead of the game.

As we continued forward, we never thought twice about the supply chain strategy. We relied on subcontractors to assemble our products and invested heavily in R&D and testing. This strategy allowed us to create a win-win scenario between us and our vendors. We could agree on exclusivity, share innovations, take advantage of key component volume, and so on.

When structuring deals with our vendors, we made sure to always be up front about expectations and get all of the details of the agreement on paper, but at the end of the day, the trust established between us and a vendor was worth a lot more than a piece of paper.

———

Then there was the LightFair.

Each year, the LightFair acted as a benchmark for where we were. The LightFair is the biggest lighting show in the US. It takes place once a year in May and switches between the East and West Coast.

The first year was in Philadelphia. We tried to get a booth to lend ourselves credibility, but we ran into resistance. The LightFair was almost like a cartel. They didn't want new faces or companies. Anyone who might threaten the old guard was boxed out. They wouldn't give us a booth, despite our efforts and lobbying. It wasn't the worst news. Even if they had offered us a booth, we wouldn't have been able to afford it anyways. So, with no booth, we printed business cards with fake names, acted like potential customers, and learned as much as we could.

We were especially curious about how these vendors would talk to a customer about the pricing and how they convinced customers that a $50 light would ultimately save them money because they'd get back the savings within 18 months.

At this LightFair, we found that most of the key players in the market didn't actually have much to show when it came to LEDs, and they had even less to show when it came to educating the customer. We realized we were a step ahead of the game since we already had a website and cut sheets in place.

Our cut sheets, in particular, stood out. The "cut sheets," or data sheets, were and still are extremely important in the lighting industry. These are typically two-page documents that specify all the technical information about a product.

When building ours, I researched other companies' cut sheets and wasn't impressed. You could tell they were from old companies. Most were poorly laid out and had unappealing graphics and lots of text that people likely wouldn't read. When we asked salespeople how they accessed information about the products, they said it was almost impossible, and then they'd add, "but that's just how it is."

We decided that it didn't have to be that way and went in the opposite direction. We focused on making each cut sheet as visually appealing as possible and added only a few key points about the product, never more than six. This way, prospective customers could quickly browse the sheet and have a sense of what they'd get. They could clearly see the image of the product to see if it was equivalent to what they already had.

To stand out even further, we also included icons about lifetime, dimmability, color rendering, where the product could be used, and more. These icons were later copied by our competitors, which told us we were onto something. Finally, at the bottom of each sheet, we included the savings and why the product was worth buying. Because of all this, our cut sheets worked on two levels. They were informational and helped us sell the products.

To align with our energy-saving approach to business, we never actually printed cut sheets. They stayed online.

We could quickly pull them up on our website or point people to the correct web address, which further helped us stand out as a tech company rather than an old-school lighting company.

When we finally began to partner with distributors, they were thankful we took the time to create a different kind of cut sheet, which would make the products look better and easier to sell.

The second year at the LightFair, we still couldn't get a booth. Instead, we rented a hotel room a couple hundred feet from the show in Las Vegas and invited people to come see our product there. Over the course of three days, we had three people visit us. It was a total failure.

The third year, in Philadelphia, we decided to take things up a notch. We rented Maggiano's, a pizza place next to the convention center, and spent an entire morning retrofitting the entire restaurant with our lights. We offered free lunch to anyone who visited and had a huge turnout. People could see our new product line in action.

The fourth year was again in Las Vegas, and we finally had a booth. We had a huge footprint at this point. The fair couldn't deny us a spot. Plus, more important to them, we had the money to pay for it. We invested what would've been our first two years' marketing budget, and it paid off. We had one of the most visited booths at the show. It was a major milestone.

By this point, we had an internal sales team across the US and a few engineers in China. We invited them all to join us. They'd never met each other, but everyone quickly bonded over the shared vision and excitement of a growing company. The first night, everyone got along so well that they stayed out clubbing until 3:00 a.m. and showed up tired the next morning at the show, but we didn't mind. One late night was worth the bonding, and to us, it was the first time we felt like we had a real team.

These shows showed our progression along the way. The first year, we faked it. The second, we tried to make it however we could. The third, we'd learned enough to capitalize on the time without having a booth. But even that first year was worthwhile. It was there, that first year at the LightFair, that we made a connection with the people at West-Lite, who'd later become our first distributor.

OUR FIRST DISTRIBUTOR

COLE

Throughout 2011, we continued to chip away at end users in San Francisco. They'd started to tell their distributors that they were interested in our product or that they were switching over and were no longer working with the distributor but instead with us.

At some point, with all this, the distributors began to embrace us and give us a shot.

We reached a turning point when one of the two largest distributors in the San Francisco area met with us down in LA. West-Lite has been in the industry forever, and they service most of the West Coast.

One of the engineers I'd met at the LightFair had taken a liking to me and called his sales contact at West-Lite, a man named Tony. Upon meeting, Tony and I quickly built a solid relationship.

He worked hard on my behalf, eventually persuading upper management to have a conversation with me.

Garry, the owner of the company, was hesitant to work with us. West-Lite had bought our competitors' products for years. There was a lot of loyalty. Garry's father started the company and maintained relationships with the same manufacturers for decades.

When we finally met Garry, we had a nice conversation. He seemed open to working with us, and during the meeting, we were able to get a list of all their salespeople—all 25 that serviced their territories. In the following days, I called every single one of them. Over half of them I met with in person, and I spent time building relationships with each one of them before the distributor had even purchased our products.

About three weeks later, I called Garry back to follow up on our initial meeting. "You really move fast," he replied.

"I can't believe you met with almost all our salespeople; I didn't even give you permission to meet with *one* of them."

In truth, I think he appreciated my persistence and aggressiveness. Maybe he saw the same thing in us that our first supplier had—our drive. If anyone was going to break through this market, it would be us.

In May of 2011, Guillaume and I had lunch with Garry, and he informed us that he was going to place a stocking order. He ended up placing a $25,000 order, which was a huge validation for the company. It proved that we could establish a sales channel to buy our products. We were no longer two guys selling light bulbs door-to-door. We had a distributing partner. We had a real business.

HALF OF THE BATTLE IS BEING SEEN

With distributors, it was rejection after rejection. But we learned that even if you don't have the best product, a lot is simply about being seen over and over again. Once you identify a target, you want to get in front of them, even before you're ready. This way, they can witness the progress and be part of the journey. Then, after a while, you become one of the names in the mix. The same principle holds true whether you're working with vendors, banks, end users, or distributors.

This is important to remember: you can't win on day one. It's no use worrying about having the best product from the start if nobody's going to buy it. You need a good product, but more importantly, you need visibility. Plenty of companies get started and even continue with poor products. Thankfully, our product was good from the start, and once we were seen, we had nowhere to go but up.

As a result of our persistence, countless distributors wanted to work with us over time. In fact, we reached a point where we were vetting them. Each time a distributor was interested in working with us, they'd send us an application to fill out. Soon enough, we were getting an application a day, and then dozens. Ultimately, we had over 6,000 distribution partners, and managing them all became someone's full-time job on the US side.

MEETING THE MARKET

GUILLAUME

We began to feel the momentum now that we were finally doing business across the seas. We knew we could meet the market and even exceed it. We also became more clear on how exactly we were positioned among the other players.

While other lighting companies were renovating their houses when they started venturing into the LED market, we were building a house from scratch. In some ways, though, it was easier to build from scratch.

The big companies were invested in lighting production continuing as per usual. They had manufacturing facilities that focused on traditional lighting products (fluorescent, halogen, CFL, and incandescent), and they didn't feel the need to gain market shares in the new technology of LED. A company like Philips (Signify), which started selling lights in the early 1900s, was doing billions a year in sales when we entered the market. They clearly had their profit source, but because they were fat and happy, their heads were in the sand when it came to LEDs. They were unwilling to push the technology or rock the boat.

These legacy companies were leaders in the existing technologies, and they had a long-established network of salespeople who didn't want to jump to a new product, especially if they'd have to convince someone to pay $30 for a lamp when there were already others for $1.50. They were hesitant to switch over. These lights were cheap to manufacture, and with a shorter life span than LEDs, with multiple repeat orders, there was a constant flux of business. It was difficult to convince a salesperson to sell LEDs with the knowledge that they'd be losing repeat business. However, what these companies weren't paying attention to was how quickly the technology was improving or how prices were dropping to a point that would attract a lot of end users.

Some companies excelled at executing a vision for LED but then lost track of the market. Despite having good funding and making a lot of noise up front, they eventually went under. Others that focused on LED ran out of business because they either overpriced their product or hadn't set a proper foundation for manufacturing new products to keep up with market demands.

While venture-backed businesses could focus on growth, we were self-funded and needed the business to be profitable. Everything was about growing the bottom line, being highly optimized with our cash, and managing our profits.

The only problem was that, even with our first two big wins, we were still barely staying afloat. Our predicament was not for lack of effort. We were each a one-man show on our side of the Pacific Ocean. We worked like crazy and gave it 100 percent.

To get to that next level, however, we needed to find leverage points in each part of the business and hire others to support our growth.

By the time I'd sent our first shipment of product Cole's way in February 2011, I knew I couldn't keep juggling so much myself. Most mornings, I'd call Cole first thing and then immediately jump into preparing a purchase order (PO) in Excel. If an upcoming product was ready, I'd need to schedule an inspection, find an inspector, and contact the freight forwarder to book the space on a ship.

In the afternoon, I'd handle a whole set of other tasks—whether it was overseeing new packaging from a designer, coordinating and testing samples from a vendor, contacting UPS, or preparing invoices to send to Cole.

We wanted to be a reliable brand, so we didn't want to take any shortcuts with creating the product. To reach the results we needed, I leveraged everyone with whom I could get involved, including friends, colleagues, and vendor teams I had connected with over time.

Of course, creating the light was only part of the equation. There was the packaging, the sticker on the packaging, inspections, and reviews.

When it came time to ship the product, I had another dozen tasks to complete as I managed all the logistics and made sure we had enough products in the supply chain. To make matters worse, the shipping industry never seemed to catch up with modern-day technology, and I drowned in all the required paperwork.

Few companies had to reckon with the time constraints we were under. If we didn't work hard to stay relevant and move quickly, we'd lose our product advantage.

The benefit of doing all these tasks myself was that I knew each step of the process like the back of my hand. The problem, of course, was that I couldn't keep up. After we received our first big sale with the furniture store, we realized that we needed a team to help us. It was time to start hiring.

Unfortunately, my first job posting didn't entice many top candidates. In fact, only one person, Veronica, responded to schedule an interview, and she didn't even show up for it. The following day, she called and said she'd forgotten. Due to the situation I was in, I had her come into the "office" anyway, and since she was the only one there, I hired her.

In the end, I was extremely thankful that I did. Even though Veronica hadn't even completed college and was working odd jobs at the time, she was willing to learn. And she did.

She soaked in everything I shared with her and soon began taking on many of the tasks that were overflowing from my schedule. I had her start with merchandising—placing orders and coordinating inspections—and she continued from there. I had no idea at the time that Veronica would ultimately become the head of the entire R&D team. All I knew was that I desperately needed her help, and with her on board, I could stay on top of everything, even when I went on trips to the US for research.

With my first hire, I practiced passing along the tried-and-true business motto Cole and I had developed together: *Look for the solution, not the problem.*

Sure, we didn't have a lab or technical people on the team yet. We didn't have a CFO or much of any accounting for that matter. We didn't have much money to sustain ourselves. What we did have was our ability to think creatively and strategically.

I knew right away that Veronica would be a good fit for the company because she understood this motto and was willing to adapt like we were. As we continued, it became clear that everyone on our team would need to be able to live by this motto.

BUILDING A
SALES TEAM

COLE

On my side of the world, I was still couch surfing while driving up and down the West Coast. It was getting too much to handle all by myself. I realized I needed some help if I was going to make progress. Thankfully, with our new order from a distributor, I wouldn't have to hire anyone yet. West-Lite had 25 salespeople who worked on commission, selling to end users. They'd help us sell, but it was my responsibility to teach them how to sell our product.

First, I put together a training seminar for all the company's salespeople in LA and presentations at two distribution centers. After the seminar, I worked with each salesperson one-on-one. I'd spend a half day with them in their car, joining them for end-user calls. Because I was on the ground with them, I could show them how to sell the benefits of LED lights, specifically GREEN CREATIVE lights, firsthand.

This time investment paid off. Many of the distributor salespeople began building the muscles needed to sell our product to restaurant chains, retail chains, and anywhere that bought lights.

In my mind, making the initial sale to the distributor was only half of the sale. After all, if the distributor came back to us six months later without having sold any of our products, our brand wouldn't be any better off. We needed to be seen, and we relied on the distributor sales reps to make that happen. I wasn't going to leave things up to chance.

Once I completed the training with the distributor sales reps, it was time to ramp up sales to more distributors. There are tens of thousands of distributors across the United States, so to build a relationship with them and facilitate sales, a company like ours needed to work with local manufacturers' rep agencies.

Rep agents are commission based and cover a local territory. They'll have an agreement with a manufacturer to own all the sales in their territory and get paid a commission only on what is sold. In short, they eat what they sell.

Rep agents typically have 50 lighting manufacturers that they represent, and they know the local market. Because they represent so many lines, it can be difficult to get mindshare from them. When a rep goes out to sell, it's impossible to know how often they're advocating for and selling your product. We learned the hard way that just because you sign with an agent doesn't mean you'll get sales in the local market. Even after I hired rep agents, I'd have to spend a lot of time training them and helping them build out distributor relationships. I had to introduce new products in bite sizes. If it was too complicated, the rep wasn't going to bother learning or paying attention because they had too many other lines to manage at the same time.

We also learned the hard way that there are several tiers of sales reps. The top-tier sales reps represent the biggest players. Then there are midtier sales reps that represent smaller companies. Finally, there are the bottom-feeders, and the only reason you work with them is because none of the other manufacturers want to.

Unfortunately, we were only able to work with the bottom-feeders at the start, and we quickly realized how little effort they made to advocate for our product. Over the years we, thankfully, got top-tier reps on board who were excited to work with us. That made my life a whole lot easier.

When we first came to market, we found that the legacy players, such as Philips, GE, and Sylvania had some of the top sales teams, but they were poorly equipped to sell LED. The regional sales managers at the manufacturers had solid relationships with distribution and national accounts, but they didn't know how to educate the sales channel on anything new. They'd been used to getting the business because they were the 500-pound gorilla. A regional sales manager could easily get that bonus trip with their spouse by simply putting in a little more effort to make a big sale. But it wasn't so easy when it came to LED.

Even if people were beginning to see that LED lighting was the future, I still had to spend countless hours educating distributors alongside our rep agents about how the products were different, why they were an improvement from existing lighting products, and what a solid ROI would be. Thankfully, Guillaume (and later our marketing team) provided a lot of information about what

BUILDING A SALES TEAM

was going on from a technology and manufacturing perspective. By going out of our way to educate, we created a
lot of credibility with the brand. We had to keep moving
like the speedboat that we were if we ever wanted the big
players to wake up.

> Education is a key part of any relationship, especially
> when dealing with new technologies or solutions.
> Someone whom you took the time to educate will
> remember it, and your work and the relationship you
> built will pay off.

To help us on that front, we decided to hire James, an
older man who'd worked for Philips for many years and
managed a large territory in California. When we initially
met with him, he sold himself hard and promised that he
had all kinds of inroads with valuable customers. He knew
"everyone," he said. Naturally, we assumed that once we
brought him on, we'd see a huge uptick in our sales.

It quickly became apparent, however, that James didn't
fit the mold at our company. At a large company, he could

hide. At GREEN CREATIVE, he couldn't. It was as simple as that. When I asked him what he'd accomplished in a day, he often said he'd communicated with a couple of potential accounts. That wasn't going to cut it, and his lack of hustle showed. There was no urgency, no salesmanship, and the excuses were piling up before the end of week one.

Needless to say, we knew we'd have to make the difficult decision to part ways. We couldn't afford to have nonperformers on our payroll, and we didn't want to keep them in a position where they could influence other future team members.

Thankfully, James left us before we had to fire him. It clearly wasn't working out for him either.

This experience with James was a helpful reminder. Connections only get you so far if you don't have the work ethic and don't know how to communicate a value proposition. Sure, someone might have 20 years of experience, but it might have been the same year of experience repeated 20 times.

What we needed were athletes. People who could move and keep moving. So, rather than going for the established salespeople, we needed to find people with our work ethic and teach them how to succeed in the industry. I could show them how to fish, but they'd need to return with their baskets full.

Many of our salespeople over the years were wild characters.

There was Liam. Liam was a distributor sales rep based in LA, and when we first met him, he expressed that he'd already developed great relationships with customers. When I finally had the chance to fly down to spend a day with him, I was excited to see what he could do. As soon as I arrived, Liam began to wing it. Our first stop was the Getty Museum. Next, we hit up a few restaurants, followed by some random offices in the area. A couple hours into our time, I realized Liam hadn't set up a single appointment before I arrived. The truth was that he knew nobody, and he was simply knocking on doors. At each new place, he'd say, "Don't worry. I've got this, Cole," and within a few minutes, he'd return and say the people were busy and that we could move on. I left that day wondering how Liam would ever make a sale, but somehow he did.

Then there was Frank, a sales rep for our New York City partner. He was something straight out of a Broadway show. When I went to visit him for a day, I realized that he also had his own method to his madness. Before each meeting, he'd open the middle console of his car, take out a comb, and slick back his hair. Then we'd go in. Just like Liam, Frank found a way to sell. And I didn't want to get in the way of what worked for him.

Both these characters helped me realize that I'd simply need to trust these people's process, however wild it was.

As we continued to grow, we also brought on some new internal hires. By now, we'd realized that if we told people that we were a startup and they'd need to be willing to hustle, we'd inevitably filter out the wrong types of people. Still, we didn't always get it right.

Toward the end of 2014, we brought on a man named Ben, who was an experienced operations manager. We were excited about what he could bring, but it quickly became apparent that he wasn't the right fit. We needed to be more patient.

In some ways, the internal team was a revolving door in those early years. New hires needed to understand what our business was and wasn't, and we needed to know that they could keep up.

Thankfully, even in those early years, we eventually began to find the right people. I was especially excited to hire someone named Emma, who managed the upper

Midwest region, covering the Rust Belt. She was hungry just like us, and she worked hard. The region went from an area with zero sales to millions upon millions in under two years. This pattern was duplicated in other regions as well, and soon enough, I found myself busy managing several people across the country who were working hard to build our company.

Combined with travel to meet with customers, I started traveling a lot just to keep things moving forward. Monday morning I'd fly to Vegas, then that night, travel to Dallas. Wednesday night I'd fly to Chicago. Thursday I'd fly to New York. Friday morning I'd fly to Florida, and then Friday night I'd fly back to San Francisco and spend Saturday focusing on accounting and commissions. Sunday I'd do office work before repeating another week of travel starting the next day.

Over the years, we were able to hire 11 regional sales managers for GREEN CREATIVE who managed the sales rep agents across the country. This allowed me to take some steps back from all the traveling, but even with our growth, we continued going above and beyond. Whenever we launched a new product, we would get our sales rep agents samples, literature, displays, and as much information as possible so that they could sell our product before the boat arrived. The sales team also continued to do sales calls with the sales rep agents and make sure they had everything they needed. I was comfortable putting all the effort in because I knew that this one-on-one investment paid off.

Our work ethic set the tone for the rest of our employees. Because of our dedication, they believed in GREEN CREATIVE. Our team had a wonderful entrepreneurial spirit, which we preserved even as we grew. The company always felt a bit like a startup because we moved as fast as possible. Our team members felt like they could be a part of something massive. When we brought people on, we expected them to work hard for the company, and those who ended up getting very involved had a lot of influence on the success of our business. We made sure to take care of those who contributed significantly to the success of the company, eventually making them owners of the business.

When we spoke to other business owners, we often heard them complain about their salespeople making large chunks of money. They'd grumble about how their salespeople took home $150,000 or $200,000 a year. "My salespeople are so well fed; I spend so much money on my sales team." There was this sentiment that salespeople were paid lots of money to get fat and lazy and not actually work.

We approached salespeople completely differently. Their base salary was decent but nothing extravagant. However, we didn't put any sort of cap or limit on the amount of commission they could make. Additionally, we didn't reduce their rate of commission if they hit a certain milestone, as most companies do. In fact, we'd even give them an additional bonus on top of commissions if they reached a high target. The more they sold, the more they made.

Because of this model, we were able to recruit top talent. They busted their asses to generate sales and, in turn, help build our business. If they hadn't been out selling and hustling, they weren't going to make it in our company, so we wanted to make sure they were rewarded for their hard work.

At the end of the day, we were really happy if they could make GREEN CREATIVE a few million dollars' worth of business and take home $200,000 as a result of their hard work. While some people saw us as crazy for paying our salespeople that well, we saw it as an investment.

As a result of our approach, we had fantastic retention across the board. We had buy-in and a culture of excitement and movement. Of course, we did lose a handful of people. For example, one of our salesmen, named Henry, quit to start a flashlight company. For most companies, a loss like this would have been overlooked. Not for us. We felt it each time someone left, but over time, we learned to let people go if it was time for them to move on.

SALES IS THE LIFEBLOOD OF A COMPANY

It's worth investing in this area with all you can and taking the time to find the right people and motivate them with the right pay structure. Here's what that journey looked like for us.

FIND THE RIGHT PEOPLE

Our first hires were senior salespeople, like James, who were from large legacy lighting companies. They seemed like the ideal candidates, but once they were on our team, it was clear that the pace they worked at was way too slow. A good sales day was meeting with maybe one customer and emailing another. They were so used to having the credibility of Philips or GE, which meant they never needed to sell the company.

We realized that to be successful, we needed sharp and hungry talent. Ideally, it would be competitive people with a background in sports. We looked for curiosity, aggression, and those who'd be motivated by commission. We wanted them to come from within the lighting business, but we were agnostic to their previous position. We knew that if they fit the mold, we could support them in their success.

...

COMPENSATE THEM WELL

A startup has risks and rewards, and it can be tough to lure top salespeople away from well-capitalized businesses that pay high salaries and bonuses. So we had to get creative. We realized that many of the top salespeople's commissions were based on profit dollars (which they couldn't control), or the percentage they made of the sale got smaller the more they made. So we decided to keep things simple and go with an uncapped commission structure. If you were able to sell more, you got more. The only limiting factor was the price at which the products were sold, so the sales were within the salesperson's control.

We asked a lot from our sales force. In many cases, we asked our sales team to go out and build the channel, creating new relationships with distributors. We needed our sales team to be extra hungry, so we offered a very competitive commission structure in order to entice top salespeople away from the competition. Over time, we were able to build a great sales organization full of hungry, competitive, and hardworking people.

MANAGING ON THE CHINA SIDE

GUILLAUME

While Cole hopped from state to state managing a new sales team, I hopped from factory to factory and region to region—Guangdong to Zhejiang to Jiangsu. By the end of 2011, we were working with several suppliers, and it soon became clear that I'd need even more help, specifically in R&D, to manage everything.

I worked with Théo to submit an early prototype for next-gen models. This caused even more vendors to notice that we did things differently, and more of them wanted to have a slice of the pie.

Soon enough, it was time to get our message out there to more people, so I hired Andrew to work in marketing. Andrew would eventually become the head of marketing, just like Veronica became the head of R&D.

With a growing team, communication was key. Not only was I now communicating with Cole, but also I had employees to manage. We'd regularly brainstorm ideas and continue conversations into the evenings to keep the ball rolling. Shanghai is 16 hours ahead of San Francisco, so when I woke up in Shanghai, I'd call Cole as he finished his day. We'd discuss anything and everything about the business—urgent matters first, followed by technical problems, marketing, or R&D, depending on what we needed to address. Cole would then go to sleep, and I'd start work in Shanghai, usually not finishing until around 8:00 p.m., which was 4:00 a.m. in San Francisco. We'd have calls during my evening, too, usually somewhere from 7:30 p.m. to 10:00 p.m. Because of the time difference, it was like a 24-hour relay race, with one of us always working on the business. We liked to say that the left hand of the business was in direct communication with the right hand. We were scrappy in our approach, and it worked.

One of the most important decisions we made early on was to put engineering and marketing in the same location.

When marketing is in the US, briefing engineers on the technical aspects of a product could take place remotely, but the sample needed to be shipped to the US to a product manager so they could look at it in person. This took five to ten days. From there, testing took another couple of days, and then discussion with sales took even longer. The whole process took 30 to 45 days before the R&D department could get any real feedback. When a product has a 12-month life span, that time waiting for feedback doesn't work.

Because we had R&D, sourcing, and marketing all based in one spot, we could develop our product much faster. With the two teams working side by side, the engineers could literally call over the marketers to see what they were designing. During the R&D process, marketing could give immediate feedback on a prototype or alternative technology, which could guide the roadmap in an unexpected direction.

Many businesses put the roadmap in the marketing department. We positioned ours between marketing, sales, and R&D. Working together, those three departments helped decide what products to sell and how to sell them once they were made. Much of this was based on product feasibility and market intelligence, which had to be communicated back and forth between all the teams.

Making a product, especially one with many components, is an investment. We spent time testing in the lab, designing the product, launching it with the marketing team, and then building out the inventory with the merchandising team. We also needed new tooling for each product and had to certify each one. This equaled tens of thousands of dollars just for each product's R&D.

Since we didn't have money early on, we created an amortization schedule with our vendors so that we could keep the cash to run the business and offer vendors a percentage of sales on the back end. What we found was that most factories didn't actually care about a few thousand dollars once we were onto the next generation. They were more interested in selling hundreds of thousands of new products than in settling a small past debt.

In the big picture, we also needed to know when R&D costs were actually going to pay off. We learned an important lesson when we decided to enter the track light market in 2014 and 2015. We launched a line with high tooling and certification cost, but we never reached the volume to make the investment worth it. When I realized so much of the product had yet to move, I called Cole up to see what was happening.

"It's just not selling," he said, and that was that.

After this experience, we made sure we always had a solid feasibility study in place to know if we should even pursue a project.

———

The market considered us to be an innovative company. We instead saw ourselves as integrators. We always knew what was coming down the pipeline and how we could use it.

For example, the chip we used for the MR16 would usually be brought to market, and then the company would approach GE and Philips with the finished product. Those companies would subsequently use the chip for their next year's product.

However, we worked in tandem with the LED chip manufacturers. We knew what was coming down the pipeline, so we were able to design our next generation of product with that new component in mind.

We ended up using Osram's components. They're the parent company of Sylvania, which also had its own LED lamp line. Because of our ability to integrate products and understand the market, though, we manufactured the MR16 first.

The chip manufacturers loved us because when they launched a new chip, they knew we'd immediately use their product. We were always their first customer.

We also had to integrate an electronic driver that gave the LED current, a heat sink to cool the LED, and a lens. We pulled together all these different parts to find the best match, which is how we eventually developed the MR16.

Because of our coordination and planning, we were essentially a generation ahead of the market. We could create well-integrated products faster.

When it came to mapping out a new product, we looked to the future, asking what the product would do for the company in 3, 6, 9, and 12 months' time. Eventually, we started mapping out as far as 36 months.

Our setup to have marketing and R&D side by side was eventually adopted by several other companies, including

Philips. Nowadays, many other companies have combined engineering and marketing in China, but at the time, we were ahead of the game, and that meant we could innovate more quickly.

———

At each stage of our business, we must have looked at over a dozen new products each month. Our list kept building and building. When I brought my suitcases back full of new products, the engineers and marketers were excited to see and touch them, and since we could test the products, we could stay on top of the market.

We also stayed ahead by getting the products that were being developed in China. Our vendors could tell us what was happening in the R&D lab, and I'd often visit them to know exactly what was coming out long before a product would hit the shelves in the US. I also found new innovations by staying tuned in to what was happening around us. As we built out our A lamp, for example, I visited a lab and saw a better way to cool down the lamp. I knew right then and there that we needed to implement that technology in the next generation. And we did just that.

By the time we launched Gen 1, I'd already started working toward the second generation. For the first generation, it was all about getting something off the shelf, whatever the factory had. Now, looking to the future, we wanted to increase the power significantly so that the performance of our lights would compare to competitors' products. We were tired of being the runner-up.

Instead of becoming overwhelmed, I saw this as an opportunity. This was our chance to truly meet the market.

To get the lights to a much higher level of power, light, and control, we had to create heavy-duty products that were built like tanks. We wanted our biggest light product to have an output of 1200 lumens, and in testing that product, we consistently hit 1600 lumens—a much stronger light output. With this product, we could make a name for ourselves as the company with the durable, rugged lights.

Securing the right factory partner was only the beginning of our work on the production end; we also needed to make sure we were at the top of our game with quality control.

Thankfully, my previous company let me use their laboratory at night and on weekends when it wasn't in use, and I
would go in with a small team during the evening and on
weekends and use their equipment to carry out our tests.
I relied on Matthieu, who was a quality, manufacturing, and engineering guru at my previous company, to
help me lay the groundwork for an efficient and complete
inspection quality control framework. Because of how
important this was, I had to do inspections, train people,
and check the light bulbs. We needed to test the quality
of light in terms of overall lighting value as well as color
temperature (color of light), the CRI (color rendering
index), the temperature of the product, and the different
components to find the best-efficiency model.

When we got our first large stocking order from West-
Lite, they asked for a specific amount of product that we
didn't have on hand in the US. Plus, it was about to be the
Chinese New Year.

I knew that the Chinese New Year meant a tricky time
for factory production. The holiday lands toward the end
of January, and when it occurs, China officially shuts
down for ten days. However, the shutdown is even longer on the manufacturing side, as many workers come

to the factory from far away and return home for four weeks around the holiday. If you don't get the product out before the Chinese New Year, it means waiting four to six weeks before production resumes and your product can get out.

Needless to say, producing Gen 2 turned into quite an adventure. Veronica and I spent countless hours at a factory in Zhejiang. We slept at a nearby hotel before going to the factory at 8:00 a.m. Some nights we wouldn't leave until 10:00 p.m. We had to keep the pressure on and make sure the production line worked on our product and not someone else's.

We ended up doing inspections on the factory floor at the same time they were producing the light bulbs. This was typically a job reserved for a day or two after the factory had finished the product, but we had no time to spare. We worked on all the inspections, testing, and quality assurance while they finished the product.

Once inspection was cleared, we picked up the lights, filled a little Mazda6 to the top with them, and raced to Shanghai, where we loaded the product onto a shipping container. The car was completely packed as I rushed to the logistics warehouse in Shanghai for delivery. I went so fast that I ended up getting two tickets and so many points off my license that I couldn't drive anymore and had to figure out an alternative.

We also had to contend with shipping schedules. In China, the shipping boats have a closing time, and if your shipping container isn't on the boat in time, it simply won't get shipped until the next boat the following week. Thankfully, we made it to the boat on time. The new lights would get to Cole in time to fulfill our promises to the distributor.

But there was still one problem: How were we going to pay for the shipment and vendor fees?

Once the products were on the ship, payment was due to the factory. The products would take four to six weeks to get to our warehouse and then be shipped to a client. The client then had a 30- to 45-day payment term. So, between the time the products left China and the time we actually sold them to the customer and got paid (a five-month period), we didn't see any money coming back our way.

Within a few weeks, I came to the harsh realization that we were out of money. I didn't have enough to pay our supplier. This was a problem on its own, but what made it even worse was that I needed the supplier to start producing the next batch. We were confident we'd eventually have plenty to pay everyone, but we didn't have the money yet.

Operating in the dark had finally caught up to us. Up to this point, we were making guesses, which meant committing our already limited capital to something that wasn't a guaranteed success. We tried to estimate the numbers, but our capital could only go so far.

Luckily, we'd set up a payment plan where we didn't have to pay the factory until 30 days after the order was shipped. We were able to negotiate for this in part because we were a Chinese-American company with people on the ground in China. Still, it didn't fully cover the gap between placing the order and having the product in the US, ready to sell.

Thankfully, we had such good relationships with our supplier that we could tell them we wouldn't have the money 30 days before it was due. We explained that we knew we owed them money and gave them a payment schedule with payment every other week. Because we had such a good relationship with them, they agreed to extend our terms. We learned an important lesson here: when you communicate early, you create confidence and trust.

WHEN YOU COMMUNICATE EARLY, YOU CREATE CONFIDENCE

This was not the only time we found ourselves needing to ask for a favor. In each case, the chance the other party would respond favorably was much higher when we communicated our concerns early. The same principle is true in life: we can avoid a lot of pain by communicating prior to a crisis.

But another lesson was learned too: we needed much more cushion than we'd imagined.

The following month, we met with a well-known angel investor who ran the company on the ground floor of our first San Francisco office. When he looked at our numbers, he didn't understand how we were staying afloat. We needed about 120 days' worth of financing based on our business model, and we didn't even come close.

Unfortunately, banks had made it clear that they wouldn't fund us until we had done $2 million in sales. So our next goal was clear: sell a lot of product. Thankfully, one of our biggest sales came just in time to fill the gap and buy us some time.

THE FIRST BIG SALE AND THE MOMENTUM THAT FOLLOWED

COLE

In sales, there are always those moments you look back on and remember fondly. They stand out because of how different they feel. Winning the deal with the Israelis was moment number one. Winning the deal with our first distributor, West-Lite, was the second. Winning our first major hotel job at Westin St. Francis was the third.

It was Q2 of 2012 when I was able to finally secure a meeting with the engineer of the Westin St. Francis property in San Francisco. I'd already cold-called the engineer, a Filipino man named Jacob. I missed his call but was excited when I heard his voice message. "I've heard of GREEN CREATIVE through a connection," he said. "I'm interested in seeing the product. Why don't you stop by the hotel next week?"

Westin St. Francis is the second-largest hotel property by rooms in all of California, so I was ecstatic about this opportunity.

When I met Jacob in the basement of the hotel, he had three of our competitor's products out. "You're too late," he explained, sharing that the hotel had already moved forward with our competitor. He told me it was going to be the biggest retrofit project in the US at that time.

He kindly showed us the proposal from the other company. The first thing I noticed was that they'd spelled the hotel's name wrong, writing "Westing" instead of "Westin."

Even though Jacob said that he was greenlighting the project with our competitor, I could tell he wasn't entirely pleased with the deal. They had no samples available, sparing only three lights for a project that would replace over 40,000 lights. With such little to go off of, he couldn't tell what the building would look like post-retrofit.

I saw my opening, and I took it.

"Let's mock up an entire wing of the property and an entire room," I said quickly, knowing that I was committing a large number of samples if he took me up on the offer.

Across the ocean, Guillaume was figuring out the launch of Gen 2. In working toward that launch, he'd sent me as many lights as he possibly could so that I could test them, sell them, and get them in the hands of customers.

The morning after talking with Jacob, I grabbed all my sample lights and brought them to the Westin St. Francis for the mock-up. While we'd charge them for it, it still was a hugely risky move because it meant taking the samples out of their boxes and using them in a mock-up for an extended period. Plus, these were samples meant for all our sales reps across the country—a couple thousand dollars' worth. This risk needed to pay off.

Twelve hours after our meeting, Jacob had his samples in hand. He was shocked. He'd fought hard for samples from the other company for months and only received a few pieces as a result. Here I was with a whole mock-up's worth less than a day later.

FLIPPING THE SWITCH

Sure enough, the lights looked incredible, and he began to fight on our behalf to use our product on the property. Initially, corporate said no because they were so far along with a competitor that was already established in the lighting industry. We, on the other hand, were unknown.

Determined, I offered to personally oversee and participate in the installation of the lights for however long it took. I committed to standing on ladders and doing the actual act of screwing and unscrewing the light bulbs.

That offer got us over the hump, and we made a deal. It was equivalent to our entire sales the previous year. It was a huge success for our company.

Of course, I kept my word, spending four nights—from 10:00 p.m. to 6:00 a.m.—on a stepladder with their installation crew across 1,500 rooms, screwing in and out light bulbs, even installing lights in the ballroom and conference center. It was a lot of work, especially since I still worked during the day. But it was certainly worth all the work.

———

Then there was a major problem. Immediately, I called Guillaume and laid it all out for him. We were missing something incredibly important for the US market: dimming ability for any building.

We had dimming as a function on our lights, with a dimming integrated circuit (IC) as part of our driver, but unfortunately, that wouldn't cut it. There were numerous specifications a light needed to be compatible for dimming in any fixture.

Back in Shanghai, Guillaume worked with our engineer, Minghuan, to create an entirely new contraption that allowed them to test up to six products at a time for all the possible dimmers in the US. The biggest headache for them was a low-voltage MR16, which had to handle a single transformer for a single lamp or multiple lamps. Guillaume told me that Minghuan gave him a strange look when he tried to explain what they needed. The truth was that Guillaume wasn't entirely sure how they were going to find the answers either. But we had no choice but to forge ahead. After taking up the entire laboratory and running 30 tests for three days, they finally reached a solution. We were back in business, with compatibility across the board.

———

Dimming wasn't the only thing we needed to stay on top of. The market was changing so fast that we had to know what to develop 6 to 12 months before it would land on the shelf. Every six weeks, Guillaume would come to the US to get more samples and bring them back for the entire team in China to play with. Thankfully, because we had R&D combined with marketing, they could cherry-pick the best of each product to address our roadmap needs.

Eventually, our growing sales team would refer certain products to us, and we'd be able to test them quickly and send back results. This constant communication back and forth allowed us to know exactly what products would work for us as we moved forward.

———

After our deal with the Westin St. Francis, the W hotel called, and then the Starwood. Soon we got calls from properties across the West, from Aspen to LA, Seattle to Portland. At the time, I didn't know it, but the engineers have a network, and news travels quickly between them. Word traveled that the Westin used us, and orders begot orders.

Not only did it push us ahead financially, but also it gave our reputation a boost. Now we had case studies, credibility, and a niche within hospitality—a fairly difficult industry to break into.

In many ways, the huge deal was the best advertising we could have had. Once you have a big job like this, you're no longer a random company in the area. People begin to trust you. We no longer had to deal with questions about our five-year warranty. We had a big stamp of approval on our brand, and we could use it as leverage for the future.

———

By the end of 2012, all plates were spinning. We kept hitting new and bigger benchmarks, and it seemed like we could only grow exponentially from here.

We also knew that with growth would come new challenges. Thankfully, we kept returning to our motto: *find the solution.*

NEW PRODUCTS

GUILLAUME

From the start of our business, I always promoted consistency in design. Much of this came from my previous work with Osram and other large brands, where we had to follow a specific guidebook for the design of each product. I learned from this experience that to build a brand, it was important for the products to all follow a similar layout.

Over time, we had a couple of designers who didn't agree with my emphasis on consistency. "This color is so much better," they'd say. They'd branch out and modify the designs to look slicker with new icons, backgrounds, and more. And while I often agreed that their ideas were interesting, I knew they wouldn't fit our brand. We needed our products to look like a family. Ultimately, one of our designers left the company because, while she was extremely creative, she simply couldn't understand the importance of consistency.

After she left, I was challenged to consider how to balance the need for consistency with a need for innovation. I decided that every few years, we'd upgrade our designs across the board—on our website, cut sheets, catalogs, and more. But no matter how we upgraded, I kept one rule intact: we needed our products to have the same look, the same overall polish.

> In many businesses, there is an ongoing battle between engineers and designers. No matter how much you allow for design changes in your business, you must know your nonnegotiables when it comes to consistency. Clear communication goes a long way. Sure, you may lose a designer or two over the years, but you'll keep your brand intact.

Beyond altering our base products, as we moved into Q1 of 2013, we introduced two new products: the MR16 and the BR30.

We were the only lighting company willing to spend the time to develop the MR16. Other players had enough people, money, and R&D resources, but they couldn't get to it as fast as we could. We'd already developed an initial version of the product by this point, but now we had a one-to-one match for 50-watt halogen lights. This single innovation set us apart as an industry leader.

Releasing the BR30, which is the lamp you see in most six-inch downlights inside buildings and houses, was also a big milestone. We did the research to see what people wanted and built our model based on that. Additionally, this model worked well for our hotel contracts because it's low glare and semidirectional.

While traveling, Cole and I saw that the lamps were everywhere, but an LED version didn't exist on the market. When I returned to China, I used the roadmap and the market research I'd done to work closely with engineers and create this product. We knew the amount of light we needed, the color temperature, the beam angle, and the size. It became a huge success.

With newfound confidence, we began to invest more time in product development, looking ahead and then reverse engineering the process to a new innovation.

LESSONS
IN HIRING

COLE

By 2013, we'd already learned quite a bit when it came to hiring, but there was still more to learn. As we grew and worked with more sales rep agents who worked between the distributors and the end users in a single territory, I began to see firsthand the extreme differences between the different tiers of sales rep agents. A sales rep's role was to develop relationships with lighting distributors and lighting designers as well as any inside people who could influence a project. Unfortunately, the first batch of sales rep agents we worked with were not much more than "walking leaflets."

My regional sales manager, who helped manage these sales rep agents in the field, began to alert me to what they actually did. We began to refer to their everyday work as milk runs. They'd visit one or two distributors per day, hoping that no one was actually in the office. At each location, they'd drop off a pamphlet about GREEN CREATIVE and call it a day. Clearly, they lacked any incentive to sell our products.

Thankfully, we were eventually able to work with the top-tier sales rep agents in each territory as more of them became familiar with our product and knew that it sold well.

As this shift occurred, one thing became clear: the quality of our people would make or break us.

When I heard that an accomplished salesperson living in Connecticut was interested in working with us, I decided to fly out to meet with him. He shared that he'd worked with Philips for years and could help us grow. At first, I was excited by the prospect, but after spending five days with him, I knew he wouldn't be a fit. His energy was similar to James's, and I knew he wouldn't be personally motivated to make sales. I'd have to be on him constantly, and that wasn't going to work, especially not now, with all my other responsibilities. So, the day I got back to San Francisco, I called him to let him know it wasn't going to work out.

The conversation was awkward but necessary. After this experience, Guillaume and I committed to stop wasting our time and only hire people we knew were the right fit for our team. It was time to grow, and we couldn't have people holding us back.

Thankfully, we did eventually find some great people. Our first hire after we moved offices was a woman named Julia, who was a competitor's top salesperson. We knew she could generate a lot of sales, but we didn't want to mess with her either. She was based in New York, and New York fit her.

After she started, she came into our new office for training for a week. I was thankful we had the new place, but unfortunately, she still wondered if she'd been tricked. When she first saw the place, she turned to me and asked, "Are you one of those companies that started out of a garage?"

I convinced her that we were, in fact, an international company that was growing, and somehow she believed me. I'm glad she did because immediately doors started to open as she chipped away at the tristate area lighting channel. People seemed to buy from her out of fear. She had access to the top distributors and agents, and she fought hard for every piece of business. She was direct and a bit harsh in her communication, but it worked. Her primary method of sales wasn't selling customers on our selling pointers; rather, she'd pressure them to buy more product. Not everyone on our sales team sold like that, but she was exactly the kind of person we needed on our growing team.

LOGISTICS FOR AN INTERNATIONAL COMPANY

GUILLAUME

Like hiring, logistics became even more important and complex over time. As an international company, we knew it would've been easy for logistics to turn into a maze that we couldn't find our way through, so we decided to get a handle on it before it got out of hand.

In my first job in Hong Kong, I was in charge of setting up logistics. While I wasn't a master at this game, I knew what to look for to get us to level one. Early on, it was clear that having Cole move lights between storage units wasn't sustainable.

Since warehousing and fulfillment were far outside either of our skillsets, we knew we had to outsource the work. Thankfully, we now had more than a few pallets to store, and warehouses were interested in our business. We found a perfect partner just south of San Francisco. They weren't an industrial option, but they were poised to grow just like we were. We could be their case study.

From our end, we'd ship the product to them and they'd package each order, send it out, and then send us the tracking number. Compared to what we were doing, this felt like an automated machine. Unfortunately, the bliss only lasted so long.

Because our systems were so weak, there was a lot of manual work and human error and a lack of real-time tracking. We chose the cheapest options, and as a result, severely impacted our ability to service our customers. When our inventory levels exploded, our new East Coast partner was simply unable to keep up. We tried to set up a system where our customers could call and pick up their orders at the warehouse. The plan was that they'd be informed that their orders were sitting on the dock, ready to be picked up. But when they showed up, they'd have to wait for hours or be told to come back later. Sometimes they'd return three or four separate times before the warehouse finally had the product ready.

This all culminated with the decision to leave the warehouse and find a new 3PL partner with better staffing and systems.

Unfortunately, the next 3PL we partnered with was disorganized, nonresponsive, and impossible to work with. Items simply didn't ship for days. It was a total black box, and all our customers and our small inside team were struggling.

Here we were, known in the market as a fast-growing company with great people and a great product, but now we couldn't even get our customers their products. It certainly didn't help that we had tripled in size and quadrupled our volumes in 2013.

Over Christmas, we decided to do the annual inventory in New Jersey by ourselves because we didn't trust that the warehouse could do it. Two nights before we were going to travel to the Dominican Republic with our families, we went to the warehouse to do our final inventory count. Armed with a clipboard, pen, and paper, we opened all of our pallets and counted tens of thousands of lights. It was arduous, tedious work that we took on ourselves.

We discovered after months of disaster with this fulfillment center that the vast majority of the orders they shipped out were wrong. While the quantity of product overall was about what we were expecting, the numbers of each type of product were completely off from our records. They'd been shipping out the wrong product to customers. Our inventory was off by around 80 percent. Ultimately, we decided it would be best to counteract the issues by giving our customers a line of credit to make up for the warehouse's errors.

This was a big reality check. We spent two days counting before loading up the trucks to transfer our product to a different warehouse. We worked down to the wire, making sure we'd have a fresh start with the next 3PL.

Additionally, switching warehouses meant we had to take the time to understand a whole new process. We needed to understand how the new warehouse took returns, received inventory, and more. Even though it was the right decision, it resulted in a greater workload for us to set it up properly. The time spent by our team handling all the issues was time not spent on value creation.

This experience helped us realize the importance of investing in the right partner. As the business continued to grow and we needed a third warehouse, we identified a much larger operation in Dallas. With them, we didn't have to worry about orders going out. Everything was fully standardized. They were a well-oiled machine.

IT'S WORTH PAYING MORE WHEN THE INVESTMENT LEADS TO BETTER CUSTOMER SERVICE

Wise investments will put less pressure on your inside team, and they'll equal more orders. The incremental costs will actually generate more business and save money because you won't have to worry about your inventory being mishandled.

The same principle applies to investing in technology. We waited far too long before administering barcode scanners because they were expensive and the integration into our ERP (enterprise resource planning) seemed to be too complicated. But doing so massively increased the warehouse's ability to identify and ship out orders correctly.

In fact, this principle played out across the board. When we had a large order, we'd need to use LTL (less than truckload). When a large truck isn't full, you can rent pallet space or square footage based on the dimension and weight of what you're shipping. So, when you ship a big order, such as a pallet, it's much cheaper to do it this way than with a courier like UPS. The best carriers that provided these services were expensive, but they made the process so much easier for us and for the customer.

VALIDATION FROM THE OUTSIDE

COLE

With our logistics a bit more smoothed over, it was time to place our focus on finances. While we were no longer a startup, we hadn't yet broken out of the startup mentality. We had neither a CFO nor a true financial vision. Now in our third year of business, it was becoming more clear than ever how important it was to have support from the outside.

From the moment we started GREEN CREATIVE, we believed in ourselves. We had to. Sure, it was nice to receive a little validation here or there, but we didn't count on it. We were in the commercial market with big cash flow, and yet we still had no financing.

Capital is the oxygen of any business. Without it, your business will die. Most startups don't have adequate revenue to scale, so they seek outside investment for the early years. In our case, we had limited connections and limited resources. Typically, banks won't consider a loan until you can show two to three tax returns and they can use inventory and receivables as collateral. In our case, we were in year three, but the business still looked risky. Our pitch deck showed our strategy and projections. Many people thought we were onto something but that our projections for cash requirements were too low. Thankfully, our investment in a relationship years before came through for us, and it was just in time.

We were at Gen 3 at the start of 2013. After Guillaume sent me the first shipment of it, we crunched the numbers and realized we'd be short on cash by nearly $1 million. We didn't have the money to pay our vendors for the product they had already manufactured or for the product they were currently manufacturing. Thankfully, we had some leverage after Guillaume explained the situation to them. Still, we had to find a way to pay them back, and soon.

Many entrepreneurs today flock to VCs to receive venture capital and valuation. Unfortunately, many of these businesses die because they focus on the wrong thing. Because we always had to focus on the bottom line, we had to grow profitability or die.

When we work with entrepreneurs today who raise significant money from investors, we make sure they have updated information on a quarterly basis (financials and an updated deck). Even though a bank will not require updates, we choose to be as open as we can to sustain the relationship.

As a business, we'd invested our life savings up until this point, not having been able to raise external capital. We didn't know what to do, so we put our heads together and tried to find a solution. The few investors we reached out to politely declined. Even though we were growing fast, they didn't quite understand us. We were a random lighting hardware company based in China, not a sexy software startup that Silicon Valley was accustomed to.

Thankfully, I had one more idea.

The first year in San Francisco, I'd walked into a bank, hoping to gain a customer. I marched past the receptionist and knocked on the door of the man in the corner office. I declared that I was selling LED lights and that I wanted to show him our product and see if the bank would be interested in retrofitting.

The man at the desk seemed amused but agreed to listen to my sales pitch. Once I finished my full presentation, he explained that he wasn't responsible for buying their lights, but he wished me good luck and gave me his business card.

Now, in a moment of desperation, I remembered that I still had his business card. As we rounded the corner into a new year, I reached out to him and asked for a meeting. I could hear in his voice that he was surprised to hear from me, and he said I should come in.

The following day, I showed him our new design, new products, and the numbers of the business. We were now bringing in about $400,000 a month in revenue and would hit $2 million in sales by the end of the year. He was blown away.

"You know what? I think that there's something here," he admitted. "The bank normally requires an extensive list of documentation to get funding, including five years' worth of financials and audited statements. And we're still in the wake of the 2008 financial crisis. But I think you've really got something here."

I couldn't believe what I was hearing, but I didn't show that on my face, and I certainly didn't let on that we were in a predicament. He saw us as a rocket ship, and I wasn't going to change his mind.

By the end of the week, we had managed to convince the bank to give us a seven-figure line of credit, which would be tied to our inventory and receivables. He told me that based on 30 years of doing business, looking at every single financial metric, every single risk in our business, his automatic response would have been a hard no. However, his gut was screaming that it was a hard yes, so he decided to take the risk. We were so glad he did.

We had our line of credit but the situation wasn't all rainbows and butterflies. We still had a looming cash-crunch crisis on our hands. We played it cool while we finalized the paperwork, saying we'd need a bit of the line but not much. Then, as soon as we got the loan approved, I immediately asked, "What would be the maximum amount that we could withdraw for a loan right now?" Sure enough, the number was close to $1 million based on our current inventory.

"Well, I'm going to need to withdraw all of that," I replied.

They were taken aback. We were essentially maxing out a credit card as soon as we activated it. Still, they had to follow through, especially since they'd already made us financially guarantee the line of credit. If GREEN CREATIVE couldn't pay it back or filed for bankruptcy, we were still personally liable for the sum.

How they imagined we could actually pay the money back on our own was beyond us. After I filled out the paperwork, it showed that I had a net worth of zero. It was almost comical. Guillaume's financial state wasn't much better. We were the definition of just getting by.

Still, we had a deal, and that deal validated our business in a whole new way. Not only could we pay our vendor, but also we could ultimately show that we were a trustworthy business to finance. When we started our line of credit at the bank, we were their smallest business client. A year later, we doubled the line. Eventually, we became the bank's biggest client and had to move on to a different lender, who could lend us more for our rate of growth.

Thankfully, our risky moves once again paid off. We now had five months of financing to stay on top of our payments. Just as importantly, we could keep moving full steam ahead.

OUR FIRST MAJOR SUPPLY CHAIN ISSUE

GUILLAUME

Even with a new pep in our step, we couldn't always keep up. It wasn't long before we hit our first major supply chain issue.

Now, inventory management is one of the most difficult parts of any product-based business. In commercial lighting, several factors made it difficult.

First, about half of our business was project business, and the other half was stock and flow (small case quantities to sit on distributor shelves so that they had stock if their customer needed product). Sometimes, we'd get a quote for a big job and wouldn't hear back for a year. Because of the lack of understanding of which items would sell, a lot of guesswork went into what types of products we'd need to service the customers.

The other issue was lead times. Our products took six to eight weeks to manufacture and four to six weeks to ship. Several times, our forecasts were inadequate and the demands were huge. As a result, we constantly missed out on sales for many successful products that could've been much more successful.

The other challenge we experienced was LED lighting as a technology. Because the technology was improved so quickly while the price decreased, we had about nine months before we needed to launch the next generation. Given the limited window, not having the right stock level would be extremely impactful to sales and profitability.

I'll never forget our first major supply chain issue, when a small distributor in San Diego ordered so much of our PAR38 product that she took out our full stock. This time, we hadn't even finished production, let alone shipped the product.

A typical production time for this line was 45 days, and that simply wouldn't do. We needed the product right away. It was time to think fast.

I spoke with the vendor and found every shortcut we could. I decided we needed to air ship the product. We hadn't done it yet, and the full manufacturing, quality control, inspections, and air shipping would need to be completed in two weeks. The proposal sounded impossible, and based on our experience to date, it was.

Somehow we still made it happen.

This situation was a huge wake-up call. We needed to start manufacturing according to projections rather than orders. This would significantly help us with our inventory management. We realized it was critical to have a customer relationship management system that could track projects with probabilities. We also needed sales rep agents to communicate quickly and clearly about large jobs. Additionally, we needed to be able to gauge demand for items before they launched. Our internal sales team helped on this front, giving us an idea of sales velocity per product. Lastly, we set up a trigger to start or stop ordering items once the SKU hit a specific quantity of stock in the US.

MANAGING CASH FLOW IS ONE OF THE TRICKIEST PARTS OF RUNNING A BUSINESS

On the one hand, if you order too much inventory, you may not be able to turn enough to cash. In this case, you must focus on liquidations. However, asking the sales team to push stock that isn't selling means they're not selling what's new.

When new generations are about to be launched, you must also be aware of the stock levels on the old items. We found that it's best to try and blow out the stock on old items or ask customers if they'll switch to this at a discount in order to completely sell through old inventory.

Later, when an operations manager, essentially our COO, joined the team in 2014, we were struggling to manage inventory. With him on board, we implemented a more advanced floor-to-ceiling stock management system. He also added a monthly review of what we had so we could know what we needed to order each step of the way. With less sitting in inventory, we'd avoid losing margin over time. At the same time, we could make sure we had enough in stock so that we wouldn't risk losing market share.

At one point, we realized we needed to extend inventory tracking to the sales team when Julia, one of our top sales-people, sold almost 150,000 of the LED tubes, when she had only sold 50,000 the previous month. Unfortunately, we didn't have enough to send her for the next month. Naturally, she was upset, but there was nothing we could do. So, from that point forward, we decided to have regional sales managers review their own inventory and provide us with quarterly forecasts for each SKU. They were responsible for forecasting and had no one else to blame but themselves if they had too little or too much in stock.

NEW DISTRIBUTORS, NEW CUSTOMERS, AND A NEW DIRECTION

COLE

Beyond the validation that came from now having a loan, 2013 was also a year of hypergrowth. That year, we went from $2 million in sales to $8 million. The following, we jumped all the way up to $24 million. The sales were definitely key, but our product line was much larger as well. We also financed a larger inventory and won some awards. Our growth was a result of a mix of wins happening all at once.

Throughout the years, a big part of our marketing efforts went into award applications. The efforts paid off. Each time we received a new award, we'd promote it heavily, which in turn established greater trust for GREEN CREATIVE in the market. We ended up in literature, magazines, and websites, which increased both our visibility and, in conjunction with case studies like the Westin St. Francis, our credibility.

It was all about finding levers to pull to create visibility.

In 2014, one of our lights ended up being nominated for Light of the Year, and we were invited to the biggest US lighting awards in Las Vegas. We still didn't even have suits to our name, and there we were, being invited to the lighting industry's equivalent of the Oscars.

Once we arrived, we sat at a circular table with a group of hard hitters. With our newfound "fame," we felt a bit more confident, but it still seemed like a David versus Goliath situation. Our company was essentially just two friends and an idea, yet our product was up against some of the biggest players in our industry—huge, multibillion-dollar businesses.

Only we knew how much we'd faked it until we made it to this place. When I told people about our R&D team, they would've never guessed the team was Guillaume. I often spoke about our marketing team and quality control team, each of which was actually made up of one person. But at this point we didn't have to exaggerate the size of GREEN CREATIVE as much. Sitting at that table, we started to realize that not only did we belong there, but also we'd built the team and company that we'd finally grown into.

Our competitor for the award was at the same table as us. They'd received over $1 billion in funding from Silicon Valley companies and created a beautiful product. To say they were well funded would be putting it lightly.

Our egos inflated, Cole bet $100 with one of their team members that GREEN CREATIVE would win Light of the Year. Unfortunately, that team ended up winning, and we remembered that sometimes it's better to simply enjoy an acknowledgment for what it is.

Still, the fact that we were at the table with all the big players made us realize that maybe we *did* fit in with the heavy hitters.

But back in 2013, beyond awards, sales, and our larger product line, one of the biggest factors that played into this growth and gave us a whole new level of validation was the information of new partnerships with key distributors. Many of these were formed through sheer determination.

Each time I planned to visit a new area, I'd look up all the potential distributors and try to set up a meeting with the manufacturer's rep. Sometimes I could, and sometimes I couldn't. Either way, I was determined to find a way through the door.

In the summer of 2013, I visited Portland for the first time, with high hopes of developing a partnership with Portland Lighting, one of the largest lighting distributors in Oregon. When I arrived, the front doors were closed. I waited a bit for someone to go through, but I didn't have the patience I'd had before. I needed to find a way in.

Within a few minutes, I was behind the building, looking for an entrance. Soon enough, I found my opportunity—an open loading dock. Bingo! I jumped up onto the dock and walked straight into the warehouse, trying to play it cool.

As I looked up at the hundreds of products lining the walls, I heard a voice behind me. "Excuse me. What are you doing here?"

Without time to think of the perfect words, I kept my pitch short and sweet. "I'm here to sell you product."

The man hovered in front of me, giving me another chance to explain myself. When I couldn't, his whole body stiffened. He looked me straight in the eyes. "You should be in the front, not back here," he said with a growl.

For a moment, I wondered if I should run, but something in me kept me there. I wasn't going to let this opportunity go. Finally, I regained my composure, apologized, and asked for a way to get to the front. He begrudgingly showed me the way, and by the end of the day, we had a new distributor. Once again, persistence paid off.

This, of course, wasn't the only time I had to block out naysayers and simply move forward. When we wanted to partner with one of the biggest online distributors, everyone told us it was impossible to even get a meeting with them.

So I didn't try to get a meeting. Instead, I simply walked up to the front desk and said, "I'd love to sell you some product."

After I was passed around from person to person, I was finally able to get through to a buyer, and we established a great relationship, so much so that they became one of our biggest customers.

The year 2013 was turning out to be a year of validation. We increased sales fourfold, and by the middle of this year, we knew we had the opportunity to become a true leader in the market. We were positioned perfectly, but we needed to focus. We needed to step out of the day-to-day and see where we were as a business.

For three straight years—from the time we started talking about ideas and preparing to launch the business in the middle of 2010—we'd been so caught up in work 10 to 15 hours per day, six or seven days a week, that we hadn't taken time to reflect and start making long-term decisions for our company.

We decided we needed a fresh environment to strategize and settled on the Hard Rock Hotel in Chicago. We felt Chicago was a good representation of the entire country and thought we'd benefit from spending time in that market. Plus, the Hard Rock Hotel seemed like a fun place to stay.

We approached the meeting like consultants and took the time to fully examine GREEN CREATIVE and understand how to position ourselves moving forward. We rented a meeting room, and for two full days, we pored over all aspects of the business, diving into the data. Prior to this meeting, we hadn't had a moment to pause and conduct a proper analysis. We made decisions based on our gut. We figured that if something was working, we'd keep doing it, but we never took the time to understand if it would've been smarter to do something else.

This time was different. With data in hand, we did a 360-degree examination on all aspects of the business. We studied our customers and how we acquired them. We analyzed our products, the sales velocity, and where they were selling. We discussed our inventory and how our supply chain ran. We looked at who the big customers were in the market and why they chose us. We identified our competitors and discussed how to position ourselves against them. Finally, we looked at the product line and roadmap to see what was missing, where we could invest more, and how to further ramp up sales.

Now, we'd always had some sort of a roadmap from day one. It provided a clear sense of where we needed to go, and we examined and retooled it throughout the year. We'd outline the item types we intended to launch and then map out the performance targets, specifications, variations, and cost. We would then map out our sales targets as well as potential sales quantities. The last thing we wanted to do was invest R&D and marketing in a product that didn't sell. But, on the other hand, if we created a product that sold well but had poor margins, that would not be considered a successful product either. The products we launched needed to be able to sell well at the right margin, and the roadmap helped us map everything out and set clear expectations.

It helped guide us with Gen 1 and 2, and it allowed us to look ahead to where we were going. If we knew where we wanted to be in Q2 of the following year, we'd know what benchmarks we'd need to hit to get there. We'd discuss the research we needed to do and what we still needed to buy to reach our goals.

But even with our roadmap, it had been far too long since we'd been able to take a step back and examine our business. The mini-retreat at the Hard Rock Hotel provided needed insights.

First, we realized we couldn't keep running GREEN CREATIVE like we were if we wanted to avoid making big mistakes. As we grew, the cost of small mistakes also scaled. Our order volumes were increasing dramatically, and making a few bad inventory buys could quickly become a multimillion-dollar mistake, potentially wiping out an entire year of profit or worse.

This hotel stay also reinforced our need to more thoroughly use our data to inform the strategies and business decisions necessary to continue scaling the company. While we still didn't have the proper reporting and analytics we would've hoped for, by taking a step back and looking at the numbers, we were able to make better-informed decisions and shift toward longer-term thinking.

At this point, we were taking market share from our competitors, but we also saw many opportunities to develop new products for our expanding customer base. After all, if you sell salt to a restaurant, it also makes sense to sell them pepper. As a team, we knew we had the potential to be a leader in innovation and a premium brand on the market, but we'd need to invest to expand the line.

It was time for a new focus.

We wanted to offer a comprehensive product line, but in examining the market, it was clear that nobody was positioning their brand as a high-quality manufacturer with best-in-class products and long warranties. Instead, most of the major players were focusing on mass-market retail. We knew that if we entered the retail channel, we'd have had no chance at competing—we weren't properly capitalized and didn't have the volume. And cost was so sensitive in this channel that it'd be a race to the bottom. Not entering retail was one of our earliest decisions, and it was the right one to make.

After our meeting, we had more of a sense than ever about what made GREEN CREATIVE different. We knew more about what we needed to build and where we needed to focus. Specifically, we needed to move away from price as the primary focus.

Up to this point, we'd always tried to sell at the same price or cheaper than everyone on the market. This was a smart strategy to begin with since we started out without a brand or credibility. But now we had a legitimate and well-known product; if we kept trying to lead with price, we would never properly scale.

We decided to focus on quality and performance instead of driving our price down. We leveraged everything we could and spent a lot of time in the market doing in-depth field research. By doing this, we managed to create several new successful products, including our award-winning MR16 lamp.

After the meeting, we also started to bring on engineers to help refine our product line. This move allowed us to begin making truly premium products.

Over time, we were able to build industry-leading products, and they sold incredibly well. Since we had a better product, pricing was less sensitive. This meant we had to keep investing in R&D, and to keep investing in R&D, Guillaume couldn't be a one-man band. We needed a team around him to grow the line and expand it in an innovative and relevant way.

Focusing on developing a premium portfolio of products allowed us to differentiate our offering from the competition but also sustain higher margins.

GOING PREMIUM

GUILLAUME

Our decision to focus on building ourselves as a premium brand was a huge turning point for us as a business. We realized that we needed to invest in beautiful, high-quality products, and we needed to understand how these products would sell.

I spoke with salespeople and customers alike to understand the market's needs. Many times, people we spoke with would mention a product, a usage, or a need. Gathering all this info was key in determining what was valuable to pursue and what wasn't. Strong customer involvement was key for new products, innovations, and patents. With this information in hand, I got to work building products to fit that need, and soon enough, we began to be seen as a premium manufacturer.

————

Not all our salespeople were 100 percent on board with our decision to go premium. They knew we were in a deflationary industry and wondered how we could keep charging so much. Some were adamant that the price shown on the SKU was simply too high. But Cole and I had made our mistake one too many times. If we lowered the price by 10 percent, we'd have to sell 20 percent more to make up the difference in margin. If we did this, it would take a lot of effort all around and lose us money in the long term.

Still, we understood why the higher price could frustrate the sales team. This realization isn't natural from the sales side. On the marketing side, it's easier to think about, but often the sales side puts the brakes on, as they find it easier to sell on price. This is *true*, but it's also *wrong*. We needed to make sure they understood the reasoning behind it. Eventually, they would see how a higher color rendering, longer lifetime and warranty, and better overall design equated to a more expensive product. And once our sales team got behind our message, our customers could see the value too.

For some large-volume jobs, however, we did customize pricing slightly, but we'd never go below the margin floor we'd set. Every now and then, it lost us a job, but for the most part, our product stood out. Customers knew what they were getting with us and were willing to pay the extra amount. Distributors also knew they were adding value for customers by offering our product line as an option. After all, their customers could always find a cheaper price, but they couldn't always find a higher-quality product and better customer service.

The proximity of R&D and marketing continued to help with development timelines. From day one, the marketing team gave input to help us create the best design. Additionally, I spoke directly with the manufacturer to understand the best way to make the product. As that happened, we communicated with marketing and worked toward certifications. Instead of going step-by-step, we moved in tandem and significantly condensed our market.

One of our first points of focus after our meeting, out of hundreds, was the 50-watt MR16, the holy grail of the LED lighting world. There were about a billion sockets in the US that used a 50-watt halogen at the time. In 2012, no one thought a one-for-one LED was possible. Only Philips had an equivalent version, but they just used a fan in an oversized lamp. With a light as small as the one we were trying to build, there was less area to dissipate the heat within the product. The available LED chips created too much heat and significantly reduced its life span. So, instead, companies focused on creating big LEDs.

When we spoke with experts about our goal to create a small LED, we were told it was impossible.

I wouldn't take no for an answer. I spent a lot of time researching leading up to the MR16. I pored over LED cut sheets and examined what was coming to the market. I examined each component and what it did. After months of research, I found a way forward. By using six smaller LEDs instead of three to four larger ones, we were able to manufacture enough light for the MR16 without overheating the body.

Yes, this process took a lot of time and money, but it ultimately got us our premium product. And as the first LED lighting company to replace a traditional 50-watt MR16, we gained a whole new level of exposure.

———

Even with this increased exposure, our loan from the bank, and our hypergrowth, we were still running into some money issues around the end of 2013 and were happy to entertain any new business that came our way.

Earlier in the year, I had received an email inquiry from a distribution company in Saudi Arabia looking for a large number of LED lights for a project. Then, on a random Saturday, I received a voice message from the same company. It all seemed like a joke. We'd often get similar emails from various foreign countries that were not worthwhile endeavors, but a call on a Saturday seemed odd. Later, I learned Saturday was part of the workweek in Saudi Arabia.

I decided to follow up just in case, and the person informed me that the company was looking to supply Aramco. I'd never heard of Aramco, but after a quick Google search, I realized it was one of the biggest oil companies in the world. Maybe there was something here.

This was a multimillion-dollar project, and it was beyond the scope of anything we'd done previously. It almost seemed too good to be true.

The whole time, we felt like the contract was unobtainable. We put everything together, but doubted we could secure a deal for a few million in sales. After all, we were still a small LED lighting company bidding against the big players. Plus, bidding for a Saudi Arabian company required its own specificity. For example, they use 110 volts in some locations and 220 volts in others, so we would have to develop a wide-range-voltage product for this specific application. To even get the deal, we had to develop new products, certify them, and send them samples.

Cole and I were on holiday with our parents in Punta Cana when we received an email: *Mabruk! You've won the deal.*

We were shocked. We didn't think it was even possible for us to get it. Looking back, what I think swayed the deal in our favor was that, first, we offered a product line that overcame the wide voltage use in Saudi Arabia, since their residential had some 120-volt and some 220-volt outlets. This wasn't a standard product at all. Second, we were a US company, and third, we managed to get all the certification and crazy R&D efforts that most companies would've never gotten without an order in place. We undeniably demonstrated that we were willing to put in the work to get the job done even before it started.

Alongside their congratulations, they informed us that they needed the lights the next day. We rented a 747 plane, filled it with light bulbs, and flew it over to Saudi Arabia. The irony was that the bulbs then sat in storage for months before being installed. Clearly, they conducted their business with a "hurry up and wait" mentality.

In many ways, the project was a huge win, but it also took a lot of our focus and energy for several months. We dedicated an astronomical number of resources to the project. Thankfully, some of that investment paid off long-term. We later leveraged our know-how to build 110 volts to 277 volts for our market since some industrial or public lighting areas in the US use 277 volts.

Negotiating payment was a whole other part of the process. They wanted to use a letter of credit, which included a huge list of requirements. In other words, they could refuse payment if we didn't meet their criteria. We ended up revising it four or five times, each revision costing a couple thousand dollars with the bank.

Until the lights were delivered and paid for, we didn't know what was going to happen. Finally, after all the negotiations, the money made its way into our bank account. It was one of the biggest and most profitable deals we ever made.

————

A few months later, we went to Saudi Arabia for a trade show, thinking we might be able to expand our market there. We brought one of our new sales managers, a man named Martin, with us since he was older than us both. In the Middle East, we'd be seen as too young to be running a company, so Martin's presence defused any confusion.

The trade show was unlike any we'd been to. The cultural differences were evident. Women wore traditional clothing, and we couldn't shake their hands. The restaurants had men's sections and family sections, and we were always in the men's. We also noticed that many of the businesses were managed by foreigners, especially Indians, and it was a very unstructured market despite the huge economy.

After the excitement of our contract and our trip to Saudi Arabia, we ultimately realized that we needed to focus on what we were doing best: selling lights in the US. Getting such a large deal in a different country was highly validating and a great learning experience, but it wasn't a long-term play. We saw what we were capable of from an R&D standpoint, but we also saw that we needed to focus on our main market if we wanted to scale in every area.

Saudi Arabia wasn't the only time we looked at an external market. We also looked at Europe. I flew to Europe at one point and met with prospective customers and provided samples. We had opportunities in France, Australia, and Singapore. We did two or three small shipments for around $20,000, but they weren't big enough to justify taking our eyes off the prize.

TIME AND RESOURCES ARE FINITE

Our exploration of the Saudi Arabian market proved to be a fruitful reminder of the importance of focus. Opportunities were plentiful in the lighting market, but we needed to be strategic. We needed to figure out how to leverage our time to provide a maximum return on investment.

This wasn't the first time we'd learned this lesson.

Early on, we decided to create a product video for our website. After two months of work, we finally had a video up and ready. Unfortunately, despite the thousands of monthly visitors, the video received no more than 30 views a week. In the end, the boring PowerPoint we used for training had a much greater impact over time.

It was similarly a lesson in the value of time and not investing it in the wrong places. Had we considered our primary customers—middle-aged men—we'd have known that few of them would sit to watch a video about lighting products. They were looking for more traditional forms of media to scan.

The lesson here was clear: know your customer, then build.

A lot of companies make the same mistake when it comes to social media or other marketing efforts that take a lot of time. Even if something sounds like the right thing to do, it's only right to do if it's relevant to your customer.

This lesson came in handy when, in 2014, a big tech company approached us with a deal. We could use their name and brand license, and in return, we'd pay a percentage of our sales to them. If we'd agreed, it would've given us the opportunity to sell in big retailers. It was a tantalizing offer, and while we'd previously agreed to stay commercial, we toyed with the idea and eventually started pursuing it as a serious option. Ultimately, however, we needed to look at who we were as a brand and what our position was in the market. We decided to pass. If we'd gone with the contract, we would've been dependent on them because people would be buying the other brand, not GREEN CREATIVE.

If we'd operated in the retail space, we would've gone after the big DIY stores, looking to get a contract for one or two light bulbs. Even with just a couple of products, we'd need tens of millions of parts and pieces. All of a sudden, we'd have needed the financial support for $30–$50 million worth of product after just a couple of months. Beyond that, we'd need a team dedicated to the retail space, warehouses over the country, and other logistic issues. Not only could we have killed our business on the commercial side by making this choice, but also we could've run into serious financial issues if we couldn't scale quickly enough. In the end, we were thankful we knew the brand well enough to say no.

STICKING TO THE VISION AND DOUBLING THE TEAM

COLE

For the first few years in business, we both did high-value and low-value tasks, but this needed to change. We needed to focus our time on the areas where we could create the most value and make the most significant contribution to our company.

We couldn't grow or scale basing our decisions on gut feelings and shooting from the hip. We were stuck in that small business mentality for a long time, and we needed to move past it if we wanted to reach critical mass. Not only that, but also we needed to spread our knowledge throughout the business so we weren't the only ones who knew what was happening.

The year after our Chicago meeting, our company experienced tremendous growth. However, we didn't grow our team much during that time. Of course, this created issues. We started to notice a gap in the operations system. We messed up a product shipment and lost the certification on a product and couldn't sell it.

The signs were there. It was time to hire heads of every single department so we were no longer in charge of every aspect of the business.

When you go into rapid growth mode, you need to build a team and lay the infrastructure down so that you can stay ahead of your growth. But that all requires up-front investments. If you overhire, you might put yourself in a position where you have to cut staff, especially if you can't grow into your new team. On the flip side, not keeping up with your growth is a great way to prevent your company from scaling. We were always cash constrained and found ourselves trying to catch up to our numbers. Our team worked tirelessly to keep up with the growth. It required a lot of extra hours and effort and a ton of stress. So we put together a growth plan.

Our investment in new team members tracked with our growth in revenue. We monitored this every three months to make sure our expectations were accurate.

What we learned through the process is that with quality people, you can do a lot with less.

When we first started the process of scaling our team, we felt we'd waited too long and needed to move quickly to bring people in to fulfill the additional responsibilities. Initially, we were too focused on putting butts in seats, and we didn't put enough effort into putting the right butts in the right seats. As we got better at interviewing, we made sure to ask relevant questions. We also made sure to test. For accounting, we administered a basic accounting test first before starting the quantitative part. We did this testing as much as we could to filter the talent pool. Additionally, we made sure that the person was a culture fit and knew what they were getting themselves into.

If you hire someone who's not a good fit or is unable to proficiently perform the role, the cost to the organization can be huge. If it's not a fit, you, as a startup, aren't in the position to afford the extra weight. We had to learn to fire fast.

If the team member wasn't a fit, we had to make the hard decision to let them go. Every time this happened, we made sure to understand why that didn't work out and why this person was not a fit. The goal was to avoid this in the future.

Thankfully, we retained a lot of the best people. There's something infectious about being part of a fast-growing company—the energy, the buzz, the changes every few weeks. It's a roller-coaster ride, but when you see the speed of growth, you feel like you're in with the cool kids. We also kept things fun. Every few weeks we'd do a company outing, whether to a rock climbing gym, go-kart track, sushi dinner, or a baseball game. We wanted people to get together and socialize outside of work. We wanted to foster a community where people worked hard together but could also hang out.

As the company hired more and more people, we built metrics and KPIs (key performance indicators) for people to be held accountable to. At the departmental level, we'd have midyear reviews to go through performance and determine the plan for next year.

We increased the org chart dramatically as we grew, but it was clear we'd need to surround ourselves with top lieutenants if we were to succeed. This meant that every department rolled up to someone other than us. This was critical for getting out of the day-to-day so that we could focus on what was most important to the business.

We believed in promoting from within whenever possible. We also believed that, as an employee, you first needed to prove yourself before we gave you a promotion. Nothing was given. It had to be earned. We wanted people who were capable of growing and learning, people who were ambitious, to move up within the organization, and they did. We had many employees start at entry-level roles and move up to department heads or managers.

––––––

By the summer of 2014, our head count had doubled from the previous year and jumped to almost 60 people. We'd reached many of the goals we'd set out to accomplish at our Chicago meeting and were set to double our revenue from the previous year. Clearly, we weren't a startup anymore.

Having more people on the team came with its perks, but it also meant that we needed even more cooperation and communication. We continued to pass along our key motto: *focus on the solution, not the problem.* When issues came up, we challenged managers to find a solution for the future so the issue wouldn't happen again. We didn't spend time blaming anyone; instead, we spent time fixing the issue.

Of course, a bigger team also meant that we needed to let go a bit more. We needed to delegate responsibility, and managers needed to do the same. To help us structure the team and keep everything organized, we finally brought on someone for HR.

One of our biggest hires was an operations manager who showed us that we didn't need middle management. We simply needed key players who could manage a whole department effectively.

Scaling also meant we needed more space. On the US side, we finally moved to a bigger office. The move made us feel like true professionals, but, even with our growth, we still had to acknowledge where we needed help.

One of the biggest needs was logistics and distribution on the US end. We needed a major upgrade to the entire process, which was why we decided to bring on a COO who'd scaled another manufacturer with skill. He seemed to know what he was doing when it came to logistics. He spent a month evaluating GREEN CREATIVE, and then he essentially told us to get out of his way so he could get to work. We were happy to do so.

On the sales side, our best agents were fighting to put us on their line and work with us. Associated Lighting Representatives (ALR) was the biggest sales rep agent in Northern California, and they were one of the first to embrace us. We had a very successful relationship. I also continued hiring individual sales agents to manage different regions and find new distributors. Because we were scrappy, we often interviewed on-site, where the candidates lived.

When it came to operations and customer service, it was critical to understand the needs of our customers. While these two areas may seem like a cost center, they're actually revenue generators if you're able to provide a better experience for your customers than the competition can.

We found that a customer portal could save a lot of time on the customer side. For many years, we operated as a black box, and customers needed to call or email us for any information, whether it was tracking, inventory availability, or product information. Servicing the customer is paramount to success, and we were making it hard for customers when it came to our logistics. We needed a major upgrade. Creating a centralized system specific to each customer created a lot fewer requests for the inside team and allowed the team to easily fulfill orders. It was a massive win.

WHEN YOU INVEST IN SERVING CUSTOMERS DURING THE ENTIRE SALES CYCLE (PRE, DURING, AND POST), YOU ENSURE CUSTOMER SATISFACTION

In our case, we knew the up-front investment would equal repeat business. This is the case for many companies, and even when it isn't, the investment in customer service pays off in other ways, like a stronger reputation.

A NEW OFFICE AND FINDING OUR CATEGORIES

GUILLAUME

In Q3 of 2014, Cole and I decided that it was time for a new office in Shanghai. Designing a new space exactly for our needs was thrilling. Since I traveled so often, I found it was best to not have a lot of paper with me. I became a big fan of using a whiteboard. My small team and I would brainstorm on the board and come up with new ideas throughout each week. I knew I wanted to carry over some of that same energy into the design.

First, I decided to use a lot of daylight. The roof was like a greenhouse because of how open it was. All the partitions were made of glass. This created an open look, but more importantly, gave us inbuilt whiteboards.

Drawing. Erasing. Drawing. It's insane how many innovations and patents were born on this glass with a whiteboard marker and some creativity and collaboration. I'd draw a piece; someone would add another. Veronica would make a comment, and by the end of the week, we'd have an entirely new concept to pursue.

Many conversations came from this process. I remember one time being on the phone in my office, watching Veronica draw a comment on the glass in front of me. When I went out to talk with her, she was so excited. "I've got it. We can make the reflector like this." And she was right. Finally, we had yet another answer, all from a few drawings on glass.

Another benefit of using glass was that we didn't need much paper. We only used one small printer for the merchandising team. Everyone else primarily used the walls around us to collaborate and create. The office was incredible, not to mention all the space dedicated to lab equipment and a meeting room for up to 20 people.

This was no small step from doing business in a one-bedroom apartment, and thankfully, the space was getting good responses from our new hires. When I hired Aaron to help with QC, I had him visit the office, and he was impressed (and this was before we'd built any of it out). Even without any partitions in the space, he could envision it with me. I knew then that he'd be a good fit for our team. In fact, everyone on our team seemed to share this one thing in common: an ability to look ahead and see the potential. Without knowing it, we'd set up a culture in the company, and it showed.

At one point, we also gave Julia, a top sales rep from New York City, a reward trip to Shanghai. When she visited our office and our facilities with the R&D lab, as well as several subcontractors, she was blown away by what she saw. She knew the company was growing, but she had no idea of the scope of the work or the energy that went on behind the scenes. Her visit helped me put things in perspective. Up until this point, it had been go, go, go. But now I stopped to realize how far we'd actually come.

We had space of our own, and more importantly, we had a team. We had specialists who did better at their jobs than we could. For example, when we had someone who understood R&D running the R&D department, that whole arm of the business functioned better and we were able to develop new, cutting-edge products.

———

In 2015, we looked more closely at the trends. LED lights were decreasing in price every year as performance improved. We'd started our business selling lamps around $30 to $40, but by 2015, their price had come down to around $15. We needed to sell three times the product to make the same amount of revenue—and that wasn't factoring in the reality that more product meant more volume. It wasn't as simple as multiplying everything by three because we also had to account for returns, stock, and shipping costs.

We realized that to stay viable, we needed to start selling light fixtures as well. Instead of $15, light fixtures sold for around $100 per piece. It was a difficult market, which is why so few companies went after it. But while we were hesitant, we knew we had legitimacy in the industry because of our positioning as a premium brand. We had a track record of high performance, high quality of life, and high servicing to our customers. We also now had a strong enough base on the R&D side that we could pursue this new line in the right way and keep it premium.

Still, we needed to find a way to distinguish our product. Rather than creating every type of fixture, we wanted to, once again, find what we did best and go for that.

We made the goal for GREEN CREATIVE to be about a 50-50 split between bulbs and fixtures in a few years. To do that, we needed to develop a line and invest.

———

Whenever I traveled to the US, I took any opportunity I could to speak with those who'd installed the product. That way, I could truly understand what they valued. When we worked on our commercial downlight in 2015, I realized through these conversations that the engineers of buildings didn't actually know the wattage inside their fixtures. They simply replaced them as needed.

Within a commercial space, you choose a downlight based on size. Usually, it's four-inch, six-inch, eight-inch, or ten-inch. On top of that, within each size, manufacturers have their own different sizes. This makes it incredibly tricky to switch between manufacturers because the downlight likely won't match the size of the fixture. We saw an opening and got to work creating a special fixture that, with some adjustments, could fit the previous fixture, no matter the size. We named it the Innofit, short for Innovation Fit.

It also had an adjustable light level. With LED, you have to choose the power of the light. Once you choose, that's that. Since even engineers didn't know the necessary wattage for each light, we designed a fixture that allowed someone to switch between different wattages. We created each fixture with three light levels, based on the most common lamp wattages on the market. For example, one fixture could function as a 12-watt, a 24-watt, or a 36-watt. Innofit was also wide-range voltage, 120–277 volts, which was relevant for some commercial applications. Because of all of this, the distributor would then be able to sell a single product, and the end user could trust it across the board.

Innofit turned out to be incredibly successful because it answered a lot of needs. Not only that, but also it was a new category of light fixture. It brought our business to a new level.

We also needed to be aware of how each application functioned in real time and how it would perform once installed. As we interviewed end users to get real feedback, we realized what was needed for the outdoor HID (high-intensity discharge) retrofit lamp.

Most of the HID LED lamps that existed were doing a terrible job of actually dispersing light. Ultimately, we decided to leverage technology for omnidirectional lamps and develop a 70–100-watt HID equivalent lamp with better performance. We also knew the temperature would vary greatly, so we included a control into the product to make sure it was not overheating.

In every case, listening paid off. The more we knew our customer and brand, the more we could focus on what truly mattered. Having a better handle on the brand also allowed us to turn our attention to some other weak areas in the business, like budgeting, accounting, and simply knowing our numbers.

A key product offering turn is extremely strategic, risky, and demanding. The investment on tooling for four fixtures was similar to 15 lamps. We'd also need to put in a whole new effort for certification and, obviously, the marketing and sales channel training. Finally, we'd need to find a new customer base. Thankfully, the risk paid off. By 2016, the revenue from fixtures was higher than the

YOU MUST KNOW WHOM TO LISTEN TO IN ORDER TO OPTIMIZE YOUR PRODUCT

Sometimes this is your customer. Sometimes it's someone else entirely. Ask yourself: Who are the key players? If you're selling a bus to a bus company, you want to talk to the drivers, the passengers, and the operation managers. They all matter, and their input will allow you to optimize the product.

The more you listen and optimize accordingly, the more you will stand out. You'll move away from being a "me too" or a price player and set yourself up for long-term success.

revenue from the lamp line in 2014. We'd effectively built out the size of business we had two years ago in a completely new category.

On the lighting side, we continued to maintain a strong R&D process with some of the most demanding quality control. We had only minor issues with 277 V, T8 tubes, and the MR16, which all rely on specific controls for compatibility. However, through clear communication, we were able to fix issues and continue moving.

Once we decided to go for it, we invested heavily in R&D, marketing, and sales. We recognized that customers to whom we sold bulbs were potential new customers for our fixtures. It was a completely new business we were trying to enter, and it required convincing them to leave their current vendor.

We used agents on the sales side. Often, those agents represented us for bulbs and a different vendor for fixtures. It was difficult to pitch our fixtures to them because of their commitment to a different fixture vendor.

We had a presentation and made it clear that there were two unique sales opportunities in bulbs and in fixtures. We created a split catalog and let the sales rep agents decide if they wanted to do both or just one. For those who did both, we made sure to let them know to be serious on both sides of the sale. If they didn't push with the fixtures, we'd lose that business to a competitor.

Altogether, these innovations brought us to a whole new level of success. It seemed the glass walls and markers were working some kind of magic. We were moving like never before and growing profitably too.

FINDING THE RIGHT PARTNERS AND PEOPLE

COLE

In a way, 2015 was the year of more. We tripled our revenue and started to scale the business more than ever before. We continued to build our sales team. We brought on more employees and invested more in people and product. We also saw, more than ever, that growth wasn't as simple as growing sales and then making more money. The more we grew, the more we needed.

To keep growing in the face of competition, it was time to bring in a capital partner.

Our initial line of credit had, by this point, more than quadrupled, and we were dependent on this money, which could be called back by the bank at any time. Furthermore, everything from finance to marketing to sales to our ERP (enterprise resource planning) system needed to be addressed around the same time, and we didn't have the resources to handle each problem as it arose.

Obviously, we needed the personal liability component gone as soon as possible. But we also needed help in several other areas—dealing with the banks, reporting, and getting through the systems. The two of us weren't necessarily adding any value in these areas, and we needed our attention to go to other parts of the business.

To find the right capital partner, we hired a banker to search the market.

Soon enough, we found a match—a partner based out of Chicago. He injected much-needed capital into the business and helped us take the personally guaranteed debt off our heads. He allowed us to shift into the next gear. His relationships also helped us work with a new bank that could provide more funding. This was a huge relief since we were personally liable for our credit line up to a third of our revenue. With a new partner on board, we were able to start professionalizing our processes. The removal of the personal guarantees helped us grow the business and focus on what was most important from an organizational and stress perspective, and we were able to start putting real middle management in place.

With a capital partner on board, we also brought on a CFO.

In truth, we waited way too long before we fully recognized the importance of a CFO. In the past, we'd hired general accountants to balance the books and to ensure that we could report to the banks, but they weren't able to think critically. We had next to no projections, costing, margin evaluation, or customer channel details.

Just the year before, we were still using the cheapest version of QuickBooks for accounting. We chose it because of the price and ease of use. But, as GREEN CREATIVE grew, we quickly outgrew the scope of the software. We got to the point where we were one of the largest businesses operating on QuickBooks, and yet we were still using the basic version. The system was breaking for us every day. We ignored the issue until we couldn't anymore. Once we realized it was time for something to shift, we looked at three solutions: Microsoft Dynamics, NetSuite, and the premium, more sophisticated version of QuickBooks, QuickBooks Pro.

We did the song and dance with different sales associates from each option, taking the time to understand what it would take to implement each system. GREEN CREATIVE was still operating in a hand-to-mouth paradigm, so many of our decisions came from preserving cash flow and runway. Looking back, we know it would have been more prudent to invest in the business and think two to four years ahead. However, at the time, we were stuck in a survival mentality.

While we fell in love with one of the solutions, it was by far the most expensive on the table for us. So we went with the cheapest version. We knew it would be a bridge, something that we'd eventually outgrow as well. But we rationalized it from a cost-saving perspective.

It ended up an absolute disaster.

We found a consulting company to help us implement the new accounting software. There was a huge amount of prep work required to leave QuickBooks and transition to the new system. Our numbers needed to be accurate, so we needed a massive amount of coordination.

The consulting company then gave us poor advice. Rather than suggesting we return to QuickBooks and try again, they had us push forward and try to update and clean the data in real time. As a result, we had a team of about 15 people in the office doing nothing but manual entries all day long for over two weeks.

Nobody truly understood how to use the new system, but it was blatantly clear that the numbers were incorrect. We couldn't invoice our customers for the proper amount owed. We had no clarity, and as a company, we were completely crippled.

Because of how messed up the system was, we ended up having to call our customers who we thought owed us money. The conversation went something like this: "Thank you for doing business with us. We're really sorry; we're experiencing system critical issues. Can you tell us how much you owe us and then pay us immediately?" We hadn't invoiced them previously because we didn't have the ability to do so, but we needed the money. It's possible that they may have shortchanged us, but probably not by much.

Months later, we were still struggling. Because we didn't have the reports, we didn't have a grasp on our inventory.

We didn't know what was selling well. Additionally, people still owed us money. Overall, we simply couldn't manage the business.

The consulting company sent us a ridiculously high bill. We told them we wouldn't be paying it because of how poor of a job they did.

We learned a lot through this process about managing systems. For one, we realized that if we needed to switch systems, we needed to run both systems in parallel. Not only that, but also it was worth it to hire more people short-term to help in the transition. Paying ten people for a month and a half to make sure the transition went smoothly would've been far less expensive than the amount of money we lost doing this transfer. We ended up having to pay people to fix it anyway.

We learned to go with the system that we could've grown and scaled with over time. Even though it would've been more expensive, it was the right option for our company.

We also thought that we needed to balance our new system completely, bringing all the data from our former system into the new system. We figured it would allow us to see the data from a backward-looking perspective. It would've kept the data separate and cleaner, saved us time on implementation, and lowered the risk of ending up with the wrong numbers.

In the end, our inventory was completely off, which meant we double-ordered product in China. We'd receive an order, look it up, see it was in stock, and send it to the warehouse, but the warehouse would never receive it. The orders wouldn't get fulfilled, and we'd receive angry calls from customers eight weeks later, asking where their orders were. When we tried to track them, we realized that not only had they not shipped, but also we wouldn't even have the product in the warehouse for at least another few months. Because we weren't invoicing our customers, no one was paying. We spent countless hours on the phone asking our customers if they had any outstanding invoices on their side. It was a total shit show.

When this accounting fiasco happened, we couldn't report our numbers to the bank or share numbers with any potential investors either. It was a huge risk to not have the right data. The banks could've given us less money going forward or, even worse, called back the loan.

Guillaume would visit the US every month, and one time we took the bankers to lunch and did our best mea culpa, explaining how sorry we were. While they were understanding, it wasn't a great position to be in. They could've called the loan at any moment, which would've devastated the business.

Thankfully, we got through the accounting fiasco, found a capital partner, and brought on a woman named Phoebe as our CFO. We'd learned from our previous errors and decided to spend the money to hire the right talent. She was sharp, quite good at what she did, and identified all the pain points in our business.

Bringing in top-level talent to take over parts of the business allowed us to focus on where we created the most value. Before her arrival, we thought that the accounting side of our business was a total loss and that we'd have to rebuild from scratch. We were fully prepared for it to take years. Within 90 days, she corrected most of the problems and took us from a position of total weakness to one of strength. It wasn't 100 percent fixed, but it was incredible to see how all it took was one talented person to say, "Get out of my way so I can fix this."

Phoebe was critical in helping us turn things around and build a more sophisticated business that could properly scale. We were no longer flying in the dark when it came to forecasting and analytics.

IT'S IDEAL TO HAVE THE BEST ACCOUNTING SOLUTION FOR THE BUSINESS; EVEN IF THE UP-FRONT COST IS HIGH, THE SAVINGS IN THE LONG TERM WILL BE SIGNIFICANT

When it comes to implementing a new ERP, it's rare that it's done in-house. You hire consultants who specialize in ERP implementations. We chose one that specialized in the software we'd chosen. They were terrible. A lot of time was spent trying to transition from the old system to the new one. The consulting company just kept throwing more and more bodies at the problem. We should've stopped, gone back to the old system, and started over, but we didn't realize this at the time.

Going with a system that inhibits your data and reporting can not only impact your growth but also impact your valuation when you go to sell.

Running the former system and new solution at the same time for a quarter, or until everything is settled, is key. If things go bad, no worries' the old system is still in place. Many companies that are too positive about the new system, or want to save money, have made the same mistake as us. Don't let that be you.

Even with new management and executives in place, we realized that we still needed three more people to manage other jobs and parts of the company. The process of bringing on our capital partner sucked up our time since we kept it behind closed doors from everyone else at the company, and the experience served as a wake-up call that a larger management team was needed.

By the time we approached $20 million in sales, we still only had a few employees in the US, and I was stretching myself thin. I'd spend three or four days traveling and meeting with customers. Then, when I returned to the office, a lot of the decisions had to be made by me. And in between sales calls and traveling, I dealt with distribution and logistics nightmares.

It was time to hire ourselves out of our current jobs so we could focus on higher-value strategy and scaling.

To do this, we needed to figure out what we did best. I knew I excelled at sales and key account management with our top customers. Guillaume worked best with R&D and top-level marketing.

Bringing in top-level talents, such as our CFO, helped us let go of a lot of day-to-day responsibilities. We also realized that certain managers or employees were really good at what they did for the specific size of the business. We had some people at the beginning who excelled at the structure of a startup, having hands on all aspects of the business. However, once GREEN CREATIVE grew and roles became more and more specialized, some people couldn't handle being boxed in to one job.

For example, we started the company by accepting all returns whenever there was an issue. Eventually our policy changed, but we had a woman in one of our warehouses that customers knew would bypass our rules to help them return product. Even though returns were no longer her job, she involved herself.

Sometimes our employees also didn't know how to scale. We started with an accountant who did a decent job, but once we went to $20 million a year in sales, the complexity of accounting was beyond her grasp, so she needed a manager, and we needed to hire that talent from outside the company, which some people struggled to accept.

We learned that when we tried to save money on somebody's salary, we'd inevitably be disappointed by the cheaper option. It was better to pay up for top-level talent because the output they'd provide us with was exponentially more valuable than the amount of money we had to pay to get them.

Finally, we had to look at scalability. We wanted to hire people that wouldn't just manage their three or four employees currently, but would be able to take on more and more as the company grew. We wanted to hire people to do their job not only today but also tomorrow.

As the company and its numbers grew, we needed to make sure we made the right decisions when it came to important calls. When we were bogged down by the day-to-day, we only had 30 minutes here and there to make important decisions. It became clear to us that we needed to find top-quality talent to help out.

One of our big holes was SOPs (standard operating procedures). We'd written a few things here and there, but it wasn't fully set up because we didn't have the experience to do it. Instead, we needed to bring someone in who already knew how to set up processes and put them in place. When done correctly, this could smooth out the process for everybody and enable more scaling.

After an extensive search, we finally found a potential candidate. He had a couple of issues, including that his references spoke poorly of him, but we were desperate.

We figured having someone would be better than having no one, so we hired him.

When he started, we were just about to open a second warehouse for GREEN CREATIVE. We all discussed our strategy for an important meeting and agreed that he'd introduce us, talk about our needs, and set the tone as our new operations manager.

He completely flubbed the meeting. He did the opposite of everything we told him to do. We still needed someone in the position, so he stuck around. However, over the next six weeks, it became increasingly apparent that he was a bit of a joke, and we eventually made the tough decision to let him go.

We found another candidate on LinkedIn who checked all our boxes. It seemed like perfect timing. He accepted the job only to turn it down a few hours later. We desperately wanted him, so we discussed why he might've rejected the role and realized he wanted a higher offer. We gave him a new one, this one 30 percent more than our initial one. He accepted.

Our new operations manager did an analysis of our business from a logistics perspective of operations. He looked at what we were doing and ultimately told us that we were doing everything wrong. He told us to get out of his way so he could fix it. And fix it he did.

Through these two consecutive incidents, we realized that paying for top talent was far more important than saving money on salaries. We realized that we needed to find killers—people that knew what it took to build a business, how to build processes, and how to hire the right people.

Every time we hired someone new, it would be a relief because it took something off our plate. That said, we still had a thousand other things screaming for our attention. The new hires helped patch some of the holes, but not all of them.

When our new management took on our responsibilities, we still worked the same number of hours; we were just able to focus those hours on important details of the business. We still had the same amount of pressure, but we could just free up some of our daily problems to other people.

We also learned that it took time to put new people in place. We needed to train them, and because we were growing fast, we needed to train them well. That said, it could take up to 18 months before they were fully onboarded and had taken on their full responsibilities, so it was a difficult balancing act of having them learn properly without feeling like they weren't doing anything. Once that happened, it freed up a lot of our time, but it wasn't instantaneous.

WHAT COMES
WITH GROWTH

GUILLAUME

Just as we got our accounting system in place, we received
a letter in the mail from a law firm claiming that one of
our products infringed on a patent. This product category
provided about 20 percent of our overall sales, and they
demanded to be paid around two dollars per product for
perpetuity plus damages, plus previous sales. Essentially,
they wanted whatever profit we made from the product.

After we spoke with our lawyer, we discovered that it
was two lawyers who'd purchased an old, unused patent
from the 1990s. It was as far away from the technology of

our product as possible. However, we learned that taking the time to dispute the claim in front of a judge would cost around $1.5 million—plus it would tie us up in a legal battle for years. Not only that, but also, as it was an unknown liability, it would cause red flags for anyone lending us money.

The firm coming after us simply wanted a cash grab. People who do this are called patent trolls, the practice of which has recently been outlawed. They knew we'd prefer to settle rather than spend the money, time, and resources to see a judge. Handled incorrectly, this situation could put us out of business.

We spent a lot of money to work through it and hours of our time each week going through our emails, collecting piles upon piles of documentation and paperwork, and speaking with lawyers and specialists.

On top of the issue with the patent troll, other companies tried to sue us as well.

When it came to IP (intellectual property), we learned we needed to be both defensive and offensive. On the defensive end, I had to be aware of all the patents on the market. I was constantly navigating these to avoid conflict with another company's IP. To be defensive, we needed to properly trademark everything: our brand, logo, and unique product layouts. We also needed clear and simple NDAs (non-disclosure agreements) allocated to every player involved in an R&D or marketing project.

On the offensive side, we needed IP on our side to show ourselves as a true innovator producing new technology. IP helps position the company in an appealing way for customers and vendors as well as banks or investors. Being able to show achievements in the United States Patent and Trademark Office, or its overseas equivalents, encourages stakeholder trust.

IP went beyond trademark and name; we actually needed to patent new technology. Of course, this isn't a quick or cheap process, but achieving a patent protects against copycats, or at least that's the intention. In our case, we found a few copies, but we didn't find them worth pursuing.

Eventually, we had 12 patents approved. Getting those patents approved took a huge amount of resources. When we started GREEN CREATIVE, we didn't think we'd need someone to manage IP, but we realized as we grew relationships with the right lawyers and consultants that it was important to prioritize. It was a huge amount of work that was different from the day-to-day of the business we were already managing.

———

By 2015, we still didn't have anyone in a middle management position. Up until that point, we'd grown the company by promoting those who'd started with us into management roles. For example, someone who started with GREEN CREATIVE doing quality control eventually became a manager in another part of the company, managing other departments as well as the laboratory. We had the same setup with marketing and R&D too.

Our China team was all in one office. The QC team would be on the road or testing product in the field, but otherwise we were all together, working hard to grow the business.

However, because there was no middle management, Cole and I ended up managing these managers. We were like player-coaches; we were the quarterbacks of the business, but we were also coaching the entire team from the field. This proved a challenge because we worked all over the place for the company and also guided these people. On top of that, we had to teach them how to fulfill their leadership roles because they came to the company with little to no management experience.

While I was working with our managers, I ended up managing their team too. It got completely out of control, drawing my attention away from other important parts of the business.

I couldn't focus on the bigger picture of the business while the managers still needed guidance. There'd be days when a quality problem happened, and I'd have to drop everything to look at the reports and solve the issue. I'd lose half a day solving a problem that wasn't where my focus should've been. On the marketing side, I'd have to help meet deadlines for contests or competitions. With R&D, I frequently ended up going to the lab to help find solutions for issues with the product.

It had become too much. We agreed we needed a management-level person to take daily operations off my plate. So we started to look for middle management.

We knew we needed someone who could guide our people, implement good processes, and manage the whole thing. Once we had that person, I knew that I could focus on strategy and higher-level matters.

We asked ourselves a lot if we should've found an internal employee to take on that management job, but there was nobody in the company that was really able to take the job. They didn't have the right skillset either because they didn't have the experience on how to set up the process, what system to use, what software to use, how people should report to them, and how to report to upper management. Our employees were trained from scratch, so they didn't have that previous experience.

The QC manager was the first inspector that we had. Then we added another inspector and another. Our first inspector became a manager and then we added even more. The person in the lab, for example, was at first our only technical person. Initially, we gave her the lab, but she did poorly, and we eventually had to take that away from her. The people became managers for the first time with us. They didn't have any prior experience; they learned it on the job. Promoting them to middle management wasn't realistic.

We also didn't come from big companies or have extensive management experience ourselves. We did our best, but as soon as you have someone that's been on the job and has the experience, they know what to do, how to do it, and what's the priority. We knew they could do a much better job than we could.

So we ultimately agreed to find someone to manage a large team across different areas. This role would be more complex than something like a sales manager. Our candidate would need to know R&D, merchandising, quality control, marketing, and laboratory testing. We knew we were looking for a unique set of skills, and because of that, they couldn't come from inside GREEN CREATIVE.

We cast our nets in a couple of different ways. We used an HR agency, placed ads, and connected with people on LinkedIn. Nothing worked.

Eventually, we found a manager at Philips. We reviewed his history at Philips and found that he had worked in all the areas we were looking for. After extensive negotiations, we hired him, much to our excitement.

It was tricky explaining to the team that they'd no longer report directly to me. Because everyone had been promoted through the ranks, it was hard for them to report to someone new coming from outside the business.

Once he joined the company, meetings became more stressful. There was a lot of tension throughout the office. For a lot of people, the new management system felt like a step back.

The new manager also struggled with some of the responsibilities in his job description. We realized that because he came from a large company, he came from a background with a lot of established infrastructure to get the job done. However, he was now in a position where he had to manage everything and come up with the company's processes. He had some good ideas, but he tried to implement them the way he would at Philips, with hundreds of thousands of employees. Instead, he was managing 30 people. Beyond that, because he was new to the business, he hadn't earned any credibility with the employees.

When my team first approached me with problems about the new manager, I did my best to encourage them to give him a chance. However, I eventually realized that it wasn't working.

We finally decided to fire this new manager. It was a difficult call, and it meant that we needed to start over. I spoke with every manager individually and explained what was happening and why it wasn't working with him but that we'd continue to search for his replacement.

Despite that drawback, we learned two important lessons. The first was that we needed a general manager. The role, when implemented correctly, would manage the team and bring much-needed experience to the company. Second, the team realized that they wouldn't be reporting to me forever.

Thankfully, something soon worked out. My former manager at my previous company, a man named Bertrand, actually fulfilled a lot of the needs we were in search of. He was incredibly good at his job. In fact, one of the reasons I left that company was because I knew I'd never be able to take his position.

During our search, Bertrand approached me and shared that he was looking for a job. We spoke on the phone, and I explained the role we were looking to fill. He was excited about it. I knew he'd be a good fit and that we worked well together. I knew his strengths and his few weaknesses. His experience in a fast-growing company meant he'd mesh well with our needs.

This ended up being a tricky situation for me. Bertrand was still at my old company, which had continued to help me and GREEN CREATIVE out by lending us their laboratory and other resources. If I snatched up Bertrand from the company, it wouldn't sit right with me.

I contacted the company owners and spoke with them directly about it. I told them that Bertrand was interested in our position but that I wouldn't hire him unless the company was okay with it. Additionally, I made it clear that Bertrand approached me looking for a job, not the other way around. As it turned out, the company was making some large structural changes, so it was a good time for Bertrand to leave.

With my old company's blessing, I hired Bertrand as our new GM. He started managing merchandising and quality control on the China side. I kept R&D and marketing at first, but eventually I handed those off to him as well.

I once again approached all my managers to let them know that we were bringing him on. Some of them already knew Bertrand from the lighting industry or through doing testing at his old company. They knew he did a great job, so they trusted him. His legitimacy in the field preceded him, as well as his years of experience as a manager. On top of that, he was a nice guy and excelled at communication. He had a lot of experience and understanding of China as well.

The whole team appreciated the transition and welcomed him with open arms. Slowly, he took on more and more responsibilities throughout the business, which let me focus on other things.

YOU WILL ALWAYS STRUGGLE TO GROW IF YOU CANNOT ACCEPT WHERE YOUR ROLE ENDS AND WHERE SOMEONE ELSE'S BEGINS

Looking back, much of what made us successful was our ability to outsource and not try to do everything. We knew we didn't want to do manufacturing, so we outsourced it. We knew we didn't want to do fulfillment, so we outsourced that too. In turn, we could invest in the areas where we could create the most value. For me, that was R&D, QC, and marketing. For Cole, that was sales and customer service.

The more we outsourced, the more we realized how important it was to have SOPs for the entire organization. Whether it was the supplier, the 3PL carrier, or the sales agent in Michigan, everyone worked from the same SOP. In this way, we were a collective whole.

On the other hand, we always made sure to clearly divide responsibilities. As we grew the team, we'd involve certain key people in specific discussions, but it was still quite compartmentalized. This compartmentalization helped us grow and

...

reduce inefficiencies. People were only involved in the calls that were relevant to them and their specific work.

We knew our strengths, and to be successful, we wanted to spend as much time as possible where our strengths were. While we had to wear many hats in the beginning, we weren't CEOs and didn't claim to be. We were just entrepreneurs building our business.

IT WAS
TIME TO SELL

COLE AND GUILLAUME

By the end of 2015, we finally took a moment to reflect on how far we had come.

We had started five years earlier with Gen 1, which was an off-the-shelf product. We simply changed the color to black. We codeveloped Gen 2 and had exclusivity of the product line for a year, which put us ahead of the game. Our third generation of products focused on versatility and were indoor and outdoor rated.

In 2015, we launched Gen 4. By this point, better technology was a given, so we knew we needed to truly innovate.

We used a full-face optic to change the design and added specific beam angles and a wide range of voltage and colors. At the time, no one had a line on the market, and no engineering team knew how to reach the end goal we wanted, but we pushed until we found a way. Thankfully, we had the money to invest in such a heavy product line.

In the end, we had a highly innovative optic with a high candela-to-lumen ratio, optimizing light usage. We could check many boxes with this generation: optical full lens, enclosed fixture rated, high color rendering, wide voltage range, spot (narrow) beam angle, and longevity with a full patent. It looked and performed better than any other product on the market.

We won many awards for the uniqueness of this line, and the product received an amazing welcome to the market despite its higher cost. Today, many of these Gen 4 lamps are still shining bright in cities across the US, including San Francisco, New York, and Las Vegas.

As we continued to reflect, we saw all the other ways our business had advanced. We now had much of our top management in place, and operations were running smoothly. Clearly, it was time to stop building; it was time to refine. And for two years, we did just that.

We took this time to hone areas of the business that had been neglected. We finally took the time to build out a robust budgeting system. In the early years, we'd thought of budgeting as a waste of time. We were building a business, after all. *Who has time for a budget?* Our conversations were extremely general. "Well, the margin will be a little lower, so we need to sell some more." This approach obviously wasn't going to cut it. Without a budgeting model, there was no way we could scale. But now, with a budgeting system in place, we were no longer flying blind and hoping for the best.

We finally moved to a SKU by SKU line projection on a monthly basis, with a quarterly review with all top management and sales. No longer were we simply ordering more if a product sold well; we looked at the bigger picture. And with this view, we could invest in the right ways at the right times.

By the beginning of 2017, we realized that continued growth would require a different set of skills. At a certain size, optimization becomes more meaningful than building and shaping. Guillaume and Cole are builders, idea creators, concept innovators. Looking at the numbers behind the comma wasn't exciting for us, and it wasn't something we desired to master. We were starting to feel like real CEOs of a large company, and that wasn't what we wanted to be.

After January, we decided it was time to sell GREEN CREATIVE.

———

Between January and October of 2017, we went all in with this new goal. By the end of the year, we were exhausted and on the brink of seller fatigue. It felt like we had two full-time jobs. One was running the business. The other was selling the business, a process for which there isn't nearly enough transparency.

Once the decision is made to sell, the first thing you do is find an agent. Usually, this is a banker, or a broker if you're a smaller company. Your agent represents you, introduces you to a pool of potential buyers, and facilitates the sale of your business. In our case, we worked with a banker.

To get started, the banker gives you a list of documents to fill in the data room. Your data room consists of all the key information a buyer needs to know—tax returns, R&D, HR, sales, and marketing data, typically covering your past three years, as well as projections for the next three.

SOME PEOPLE LIKE TO BUILD, AND OTHERS LIKE TO MANAGE

At some point, it simply felt like we didn't know what else we could do to keep moving ahead. We were used to going fast and loving the speed, but getting to the next stage would require someone who liked tweaking the car ever so slightly to improve its racing abilities.

This is an important difference, and it's worth considering. Most people aren't both builders and managers. It's not better to be one or the other, but it certainly does help to know where you end and someone else begins.

Your data room tells the story of where you've been and where you're headed. Even when selling, it is essential to look toward the future and map out how you'll continue to grow. People don't buy the past; they buy the future.

Your agent, or banker, will also help you build the confidential information memorandum (CIM), which is a comprehensive deck, usually around 100 slides. Your CIM highlights your company, its key people, any relevant data, the organizational structure, why your industry is amazing, and why your company is going to continue to be successful.

Buyers also like to see audited, or at least reviewed, historical financial statements. While you're putting together your data room and CIM, a third party is hired to create a quality of earnings report to validate and audit the authenticity of your numbers. This, as well, goes into the data room.

Meanwhile, there's a lot of simultaneously moving parts here. You start creating an anonymized highlight of your business that covers your industry and the broader details required for potential buyers to decide if they want to sign an NDA to gain access to the CIM and the data room.

This teaser is usually sent to a mix of private equity (PE) and strategic buyers. PE firms are selected based on the size of your company and their mandate. They're buying to resell. They want to see a plan to increase the value of the business at the time. Strategic buyers are typically competitors, or players in adjacent industries. They might be interested based on your product portfolio, customers, R&D capabilities, or other specific items. When exploring a strategic acquisition, you must be careful with whom you go out to because they'll be gaining access to confidential information, which can be a problem if the deal falls through.

Of the maybe 100 potential buyers you go out to, around 30 will sign the NDA. Of this group, maybe ten end up making an indication of interest, or IOI. The IOI precedes the LOI (letter of intent). It indicates a nonbinding interest in acquiring your company. At this point, you narrow the field and select the ones you're most interested in. After that, it's time for the road show.

These are long meetings, sometimes two or three hours, where you go through a deck tailored to their interest and answer any questions they might have. After the meeting, they decide if they're going to make an LOI. Hopefully, you get several and you can begin negotiating with the interested parties. Once you agree to terms, you sign an agreement of exclusivity with one buyer, for around 45 to 90 days, during which they have time for due diligence.

Due diligence begins with the data room, and they can ask for additional materials at this stage. They visit your offices and facilities and meet with key customers, executives, and vendors. It's the equivalent of having two jobs—one managing the business and the other working closely with the buyer to handle all their requests and organize communications. At this point, nothing is certain. Until money's in the bank account, nothing is done.

What we learned during this time was that you can have a fantastic business and even a motivated buyer, but selling will still take time. It seemed that no matter how many questions we answered, the buyers had more, and there were other parties—bankers, lawyers, accountants—who needed answers to the same questions.

We wondered if the sale would ever really happen or if we were going in circles for nothing. But at this point, we'd invested so much time in it, we had to see it through. Like so much of our experience, we needed to persist.

AN END AND A BEGINNING

GUILLAUME

Finally, in early October, we had a deal.

At the time, we were still on our two sides of the world, where we'd started the company. My wife was due to give birth any day. In fact, she had a C-section scheduled for the upcoming weekend.

After all the meetings, all the interviews, and all the documentation, I finally got the call. Not for the baby, but for the sale of the business. The buyer was ready to move forward. I called Cole, and we discussed how we'd manage the final negotiations over the phone.

Cole wouldn't have it. After launching GREEN CRE-ATIVE from scratch in 2010 and taking it from a startup to a business valued at over nine figures, this critical juncture in our partnership was too big, too important, for us to handle apart. We'd started the company together—the logo itself was made up of our interlocking initials—and we were going to finish the journey together too.

"I'm going to come there," Cole finally said, realizing I didn't have the option to travel. Within a few hours, he was on a plane from San Francisco to China. As soon as he landed, it was time to get to work.

As my wife rested, we commandeered a room in our Shanghai apartment, turning a bedroom into a make-shift command post for closing the deal. The buyer was located in St. Louis, and with the 13-hour time difference, we had to work through the night and into the early morning if there was any hope of closing the deal by Friday so I could be by my wife's side when our child was born.

That week, we talked to over 30 people from California, Chicago, New York, and other cities and countries. We worked around the clock, taking turns with the paper-work and taking relay naps to make sure one of us was always available.

By Friday night, just when we thought we'd close the deal, there was somehow still more to do. We stayed at it until 4:00 a.m., on call after call with the buyers, the bankers, the lawyers, the accountants, the tax people. Finally, we realized it wasn't going to happen that night, and we both passed out from sheer exhaustion.

A couple of hours later, my wife knocked on the door.

"Take me to the hospital, Guillaume," she said. "It's time."

Our son was born on Saturday, September 30, and the four of us—my wife, our daughter, our new baby boy, and me—spent much of the weekend together at the hospital. But by Monday night, it was time to get back to work.

Cole and I picked up where we'd left off with the sale discussions. By then, most of the hard work had been done, so after just a couple of hours, the final paperwork was approved and signed.

After seven years, a lot of adventures, and plenty of mistakes, we'd gone from a couple of friends with a bright idea to entrepreneurs and business owners who'd created a multimillion-dollar global enterprise. And now we'd sold it.

WHAT YOU CAN'T PREPARE FOR

COLE AND GUILLAUME

From the busy streets of Shanghai—finding each other and starting a business with no entrepreneurial experience—to navigating a competitive market using complementary skills and a few bucks to our names, it's been amazing to look back on it all through the process of writing this book.

We never could have foreseen building a strong R&D and supply chain in China and becoming a leader in the US commercial market for LED lights. We never could have foreseen becoming a premium, award-winning

— FLIPPING THE SWITCH —

brand. After all, we always seemed to lack what the others had: funds, IP, sales, HR, inventory, ERP, finance. You name it.

But what we lacked in experience, we made up for with *determination* (the stubbornness to keep going no matter what), *open-mindedness* (always ready to learn and grow and change), and *teamwork* (supporting each other each step of the way).

We learned so much through this whole process and kept learning all the way through the end. Selling was a huge victory after ten months of stress—interacting with so many people from the buyer side as well as key people on the team. However, we knew it was just a step.

We wanted to have a seamless handover and full commitment from the whole team. We wanted the business to be successful in the long term. We valued what we'd built, and we didn't want it to flop once we were out of the picture. Thankfully, with a lot of continued effort and communication, we reached a place where we felt we could truly let go.

At this point, we were more than familiar with taking big steps. But this felt different. There would've been no way to prepare for it. When everything you've worked so hard to build is out of your hands, it feels like you're missing something. There's an emptiness that lingers for a time...until there's another spark.

FINAL NOTE TO THE READER

Wherever you are in your journey, we hope you found something in the story that is relevant to you and your entrepreneurial adventure.

Which factors were the most important in our journey is hard to say, but if we could leave you with three things critical to your business, they would be the following:

1. Whenever you run into a problem, regardless of the size, focus on the solution. By focusing 95 percent of your energy on fixing the problem and finding the proper solution and only 5 percent on doing a postmortem to understand why the problem happened, you can keep your momentum while still avoiding similar issues in the future.

2. In the beginning and the scale-up stage, experimentation is critical. You are flying a plane while building it at the same time. Many of the decisions you make will be incorrect, but if your process allows for a quick adjustment, you can continue forward progress despite the obstacles.

3. The journey is a marathon with hurdles placed randomly throughout the course and not a sprint on a beautifully landscaped track. Learning how to pace yourself and best leverage momentum is key.

Whatever you have to do, keep moving. Find your "race to the sockets" and go for it. Don't stop. Stay ahead. Stay strategic. And soon enough, you'll find yourself exactly where you want to be.